Barbara
Marlowe

EXPLORING
Natural
CHINA

EVANS
MITCHELL
BOOKS

First published in the
United Kingdom in 2010 by:
Evans Mitchell Books
54 Baker Street
London W1U 7BU
United Kingdom
www.embooks.co.uk

Design by:
Darren Westlake
TU ink Ltd, London
www.tuink.co.uk

British Library Cataloguing in Publication Data.
A CIP record of this book is available
on request from the British Library.

ISBN: 978-1-901268-41-6

Printed in China

FSC
Mixed Sources
Product group from well-managed
forests, controlled sources and
recycled wood or fiber
Cert no. SGS-COC-003548
www.fsc.org
© 1996 Forest Stewardship Council

EXPLORING
Natural
CHINA

HEATHER ANGEL

ACKNOWLEDGEMENTS

Many people helped in the production of this book and together they made an ambitious project possible. My grateful thanks to you all.

Tailor-made itineraries with my own guide, transport and driver were arranged by Kate Jia (Jia Min) of China Bird Tours, Michelle Yang (Yang Wen Ying) of Yunnan Overseas Travel Corporation and Pan Shijun of Guilin Photo Tours. I also travelled with Joe Van Os Photo Safaris, Naturetrek and Sunbird.

The guides below answered endless queries and together with the drivers helped me achieve my goals – sometimes against long odds:
Tangjiahe Jing Zhong (*aka* Zorro), Li Ying, Mr Yang and Mr Zhou (driver)
Bamboo Sea Jing Zhong (*aka* Zorro) and Mr Zhou (driver)
Qinghai Hu Mr Rong Guo Cheng
Puzhehei Sunny
Pandas Joe Van Os and Michael Deng
Tengchong & Gaoligongshan Emma Xuchun, Mr Ling Rusu and Mrs Ling Josi
Guilin & Yangshuo Pan Shijun
Plant hunting in Sichuan John Shipton (Naturetrek), Jason Lees (Haiwei Trails) and Ardong (driver)
Xishuangbanna Sam Yan Zhuang Xiang
Tigers Joe Van Os and Michael Deng
Hong Kong Professor A. Gray Williams, Allen To, Vivian Fu and Rupert McCowan at the HK branch of the RGS
Huangshan April Yao, Ray Tseng
Wulingyuan Nie Bai (David).

For the **Back from the Brink** section I am grateful to: Sandra Dong and James Xiang; Mr Lu Shunqing for access to the Anhui Research Centre of Chinese Alligator Reproduction and Mr Wang Renping for showing me around the enclosures; Professor Li Shu Fang for access to the Institute of Chinese Sturgeon and Wang Shitao for explaining the exhibits; Mr Wang, manager of the National Ibis Breeding Centre, who appointed Mr Wang Bao Ling as my guide for the wild ibis; and Mr Shun for information about breeding giant salamanders.

Donna Xiao provided several useful biological contacts and assisted with forwarding Back from the Brink copy to experts in their field.

Kate Carter and Valerie West assisted with typing and proof-reading the copy. Ed Pugh helped with the digital side and compiled draft maps from multifarious sources – a great team effort.

Caroline Taggart did sterling work editing my copy – sometimes dispatched from remote parts of China – down to a crisper length; Darren Westlake at TU ink has produced a design that showcases China's natural world to optimum effect and Julie Cornish has produced stylistic versions of the final maps. I am indebted to Harry Ricketts, who had the faith to publish my first book way back in 1972 and who suggested this idea to Evans Mitchell Books.

Finally, special thanks go to my husband, Martin Angel, who, as always, encouraged me throughout and accompanied me on the plant-hunting trip to Sichuan.

4

CONTENTS

RUSSIA

KAZAKHSTAN

MONGOLIA

HEILONGJIANG
Harbin

JILIN
Changchun

INNER MONGOLIA AR

Shenyang

LIAONING

NORTH KOREA

Urumqi

XINJIANG UYGUR AR

GANSU

Hohhot

Beijing

Tianjin

HEBEI

Yellow River

NINGXIA AR

Yinchuan

Taiyuan

Shijiazhuang

SHANXI

Jinan

SHANDONG

SOUTH KOREA

Xining

QINGHAI

Lanzhou

Xi'an

SHAANXI

Zhengzhou

HENAN

JIANGSU

TIBET AR

Lancang River

Yarlung Tsangpo River

Nujiang River

Lhasa

NEPAL

BHUTAN

CHONGQING

Yangtze River

HUBEI

Wuhan

Hefei

ANHUI

Nanjing

Shanghai

Hangzhou

SICHUAN

Chengdu

Chongqing

Nanchang

ZHEJIANG

JIANGXI

INDIA

BANGLADESH

Changsha

HUNAN

GUIZHOU

Guiyang

Kunming

YUNNAN

Pearl River

GUANGXI AR

Nanning

Fuzhou

FUJIAN

Taipei

TAIWAN

GUANGDONG

Guangzhou

HONG KONG SAR
MACAU SAR

MYANMAR

LAOS

VIETNAM

Haikou

HAINAN

INTRODUCTION

A century or more ago the route from the West to China was tortuous. The plant hunter E. H. Wilson had to take a boat from Britain to the United States, which he crossed by train to reach San Francisco. Here, he boarded another ship for a month's voyage to Shanghai. Now a direct flight from the UK takes less than 12 hours.

Before setting foot in any country we have our own conceptions. In the case of China, these are predictably of a land where pandas live, where bamboo grows and where rapid economic expansion has created pollution problems at the expense of the environment. All are true, but these are minute dots on the vast canvas that is China – a country like no other – which continues to lure me back to explore it in more depth.

A common misconception is that China has not developed as quickly as the West. Few people realise that for 1,500 years it led the world with its scientific inventions and discoveries. The origin of silk, the structure of snowflakes, the invention of paper-making, gunpowder, the wheel, the umbrella, the stirrup and the decimal system are just a few of the many innovations that came from China.

It was also highly sophisticated in the realm of art. Before the invention of paper, Chinese artists portrayed their appreciation of the natural world by painting on silk. Later came the exquisite scrolls of ink-brush landscape paintings, as well as flowers and iconic animals such as the panda, the crane (the ancient symbol for longevity) and the tiger (the symbol of courage and power). The crane, fish and plants are also portrayed as sculptures or pebble mosaics in classical Chinese gardens. Yet this great land of invention failed to capitalise on its rich knowledge and for many years it was left behind by the West.

Recent economic expansion has brought changes to China which have had a detrimental effect on the environment. However, the impact of water, air pollution and deforestation leading to soil erosion and flooding is gradually being redressed. The 2008 Beijing Olympics provided the impetus for change and showed what can be done to clean up air quality – not just for the international athletes and visitors but also for local people and wildlife. When more than 4,000 people died in 1998 as a result of floods blamed on deforestation, China implemented a widespread ban on logging. One million forest workers who used to earn their living by logging now plant trees on a vast scale on 135 state-run forest farms.

No matter where you turn to look at China's statistics, they are invariably noteworthy: from being the most populous country on earth (1.3 billion people) to being the largest country in the world to use a single time zone. China contains one-eighth of the world's plant species and nearly twice as many (some 32,000) as the continental United States, to which it roughly equates in area. New discoveries continue to be made: as recently as 1955 science identified the endemic and endangered Cathay silver fir (*Cathaya argyrophylla*), referred to by Chinese botanists as the giant panda of the plant kingdom.

Leaving aside the giant panda, which has a chapter here all to itself, 10 per cent of the world's vertebrates live in China. There are over 1,300 species of birds, including 62 pheasants and their allies. Good sightings of wild resplendent pheasants are rare, since when suddenly faced with a person appearing along a track they tend to scuttle off into the nearest clump of bamboo. Closer approaches are possible when they are fed in the open by the local people, as they are at some Tibetan monasteries.

This richness of China's flora and fauna relates to the great diversity of climate, terrain and habitat in a country that spans almost 36° of latitude. In the cold north-east, where snow lingers until late May, the growing season is short. Further south, subtropical forests abound and, in the far south of Yunnan, remnants of tropical rainforest can be found in a balmy climate with an average temperature of about 19° C (69° F). Within each of these and other habitat types, the flora and fauna have adapted to the climate and the terrain as well as to their competitors – grazers, browsers or predators – resulting in a complex set of food chains. In a country which embraces such diversity, it is appropriate that some of China's biodiverse hotspots are highlighted in this book; in particular the Three Parallel Rivers in Yunnan and Wolong in Sichuan – just two of 38 World Heritage Sites in China designated by UNESCO.

China is so vast that it is impractical to visit more than a few places in a single trip. But what you see and read here I have experienced – often more than once – every step of the way. Each journey has been a journey of discovery, for however carefully I did my research, inevitably changes had to be made to the itinerary as unforeseen circumstances arose. Hardly a trip passed without long hold-ups or even detours having to be made because of major road repairs.

But these inconveniences paled into insignificance in the wilder parts, where I met many charming people, always intrigued as to why a mature yet active lady should be travelling on her own to remote parts of their country.

Travelling around China I have been encouraged on several counts. Notably by the captive-breeding and reintroduction work being done with some endangered species: five of these are featured in a special section towards the end of the book. It was gratifying to see how well Père David's deer are doing in a reserve north of Shanghai after their reintroduction from the other side of the world, long after the wild deer were exterminated from China. I also met people who were beavering away to raise awareness in their local area about the need to protect wildlife under threat. Biologists and conservationists have realised the need to plant natural corridors to link up fragmented reserves, allowing wildlife to move freely from one to another to feed and maybe find a mate. This has already begun to be implemented for some of the smaller panda reserves and is also proposed in Xishuangbanna National Nature Reserve in the far south of Yunnan.

But with the majority of urban Chinese living in high-rise flats, what the country really needs is the equivalent of David Attenborough enthusing to millions of television viewers about the glorious wilder parts of their country; at the same time stressing that they will not be there for future generations to enjoy unless everyone plays their part in helping to conserve reserves threatened by the encroachment of roads, housing and tourist hotels.

Another encouraging thing, though, is that many of the younger generation appear to be switched on to the concepts of environmental protection, biodiversity and global warming. At Qinghai Lake, I met a teacher who had brought a large group of 13–14 year olds on a study weekend. When she learnt why I was in China, she asked if I would talk to them. After I had done so, they bombarded me with questions in excellent English (Chinese children now start learning English at the age of five). They were clearly concerned about the future welfare of the natural environment of their country – a country which, in the hands of young people like these, will surely continue to enthral and fascinate for centuries to come.

< Sun spotlights grassland from the Qinghai –Tibet train.

v Overwintering whooper swan (*Cygnus cygnus*) calls as it runs at dusk in Rongcheng Swan Natural Reserve, Shandong.

PHOTOGRAPHIC NOTE

Because I was constantly on the move in the field, my basic equipment was minimal. I always carried one camera body, with 24–120mm, 105mm macro and 80–400mm lenses plus a tripod, flash, reflector and diffuser. The 500mm lens was added only when I planned to visit bird colonies, as at Qinghai Lake. The D3 camera enabled me to get shots that would never have been possible with previous Nikon digital cameras. The greatly improved sensor allows the ISO to be increased, thereby providing fast shutter speeds in poor light, yet retaining the image quality. This proved invaluable in the Xishuangbanna rainforest, where I worked on the hoof using a hand-held camera to take the gibbons.

Cameras and lenses
- Nikon D3 digital cameras
- Nikon AF-S Nikkor 12–24mm f4 G ED zoom lens
- Nikon AF-S Nikkor 24–120mm f3.5/5.6 G zoom lens
- Nikon AF-S VR105mm f2.8 G Micro-Nikkor lens
- Nikon AF 70-180mm f4.5-5.6 Micro-Nikkor lens
- Nikon AFVR Nikkor 80–400mm f4.5–5.6 D zoom lens
- Nikon AF-S Nikkor f4 D 500mm lens.

Other equipment
- ScanDisc Extreme IV 4GB CF cards
- Nikon SB-800 speedlight
- Stofen flash diffuser
- Visible Dust Arctic Butterfly® 724 (Brite) sensor brush
- GigaVu Sonic 120GB hard drive to back-up images
- Gitzo GT3540 Carbon 6X tripod
- Gitzo G1475M ball head
- Really Right Stuff BH-55 ball head
- Lastolite reflectors and diffusers
- Cameramac waterproof cover
- Umbrella attached to flexi-arm on tripod
- Tripod leg warmers.

CHAPTER 1

TREKKING IN TANGJIAHE

One moment it stood at the edge of a cave high up a cliff. The next it ran down the rock face, landing on a ledge with some scrub. Quickly reorienting itself for the second stage of the descent, it raced down the vertical cliff onto a boulder, leapt off into the edge of the river and ran up a slope before disappearing into the forest. This was my first encounter with a wild Chinese goral, an amazingly agile goat antelope that can move like greased lightning up and down rocky terrain.

< A Chinese goral begins a speedy descent down a sheer rock face in Tangjiahe NNR, which has an elevation that ranges from 1,150 to 3,864 m (3,773–12,677 ft).

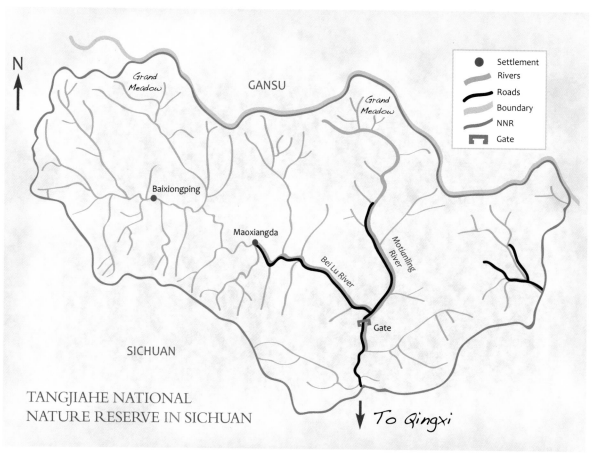

N

Grand
Meadow

GANSU

Grand
Meadow

Baixiongping

Maoxiangda

Bei Lu River

Motianling
River

Gate

	Settlement
	Rivers
	Roads
	Boundary
	NNR
	Gate

SICHUAN

TANGJIAHE NATIONAL
NATURE RESERVE IN SICHUAN

To Qingxi

Tangjiahe National Nature Reserve (NNR) is a mountain area that lies just inside Sichuan Province, contiguous with Baishuijiang NNR in Gansu Province to the north. Famous for the great diversity of its mammals, it also has impressive lists of birds and plants. While I was working in the Bamboo Sea (see Chapter 2), my guide Zorro told me about a trip he had made to Tangjiahe a few months earlier with an enthusiastic mammal-tracker from Australia. After more research back home, I was intrigued enough to draft an itinerary and request Zorro as my guide.

Leaving Chengdu, the capital of Sichuan, in mid-October, we sped north-east along an expressway for the first 200 km (125 miles); thereafter, progress was much slower as we had to cope with roads damaged by the 2008 earthquake and endless lorries loaded with

< White-throated laughing thrushes (*Garrulax albogularis*) move through the forests in flocks, feeding on insects, berries and seeds.

bricks, stones, sand or pipes. The saddest sight was the cluster of crude wooden crosses erected atop a few mounds in memory of all the children lost in a primary school in Dong He Kou, a village that had been completely flattened by the collapse of a huge hillside. With not a single house left standing, the newly built, capacious yet empty parking lot – complete with a row of vendors' kiosks – appeared incongruous, until Zorro told me it was a stopping point on a popular tour to view the devastated areas.

Inside the reserve gate, we negotiated more earth-moving vehicles and road works. While waiting for a lane to be cleared we were interrogated about why we wanted to visit the reserve, because the area was closed to general tourists so that the road could be rebuilt. On learning I was a foreigner, the authorities gave us special permission to enter, waving us through with big smiles. Apart from a British film

^ A Sichuan takin pauses as it feeds in the late afternoon, showing the curiously shaped horns that rise from the centre of the massive head, curving outwards, backwards and upwards before ending in a point.

crew who stayed for a couple of nights, I was the sole guest in the hotel inside the reserve.

Initially the road follows the Tangjiahe River, which splits into two; the left-hand fork becomes the Bei Lu River, which flows beside the hotel. As we approached the hotel, late in the afternoon, I had my first sighting of a Sichuan takin (*Budorcas taxicolor tibetana*) grazing out in the open on a grassy slope facing the road.

Takin are curious-looking, stocky goat antelopes, with a coat that changes colour with age. Babies have dark fur which gradually lightens to gold as they mature. Could it be that the legend of the 'golden fleece', searched for by Jason and the Argonauts, was inspired by the takin's lustrous coat?

^ Maples are among the many deciduous trees whose leaves add a riot of colour to the mixed forests in Tangjiahe during autumn.

⌐ A river chat or white-capped water-redstart (*Chaimarrornis leucocephalus*) is frequently seen on rocks beside the mountain streams, bobbing its head.

>> *Sorbus hupehensis*, related to the European mountain ash (*S. aucuparia*), is unusual in producing clusters of white berries. These contrast with foliage that ultimately turns a fiery red.

In spite of weighing over 350 kg (790 lb), takin are remarkably agile climbers, able to run up and down steep mountain slopes. The best time to see them is in summer, when they congregate in large groups in the alpine meadows above 3,000 m (10,000 ft), grazing on the more palatable grasses and seeking refuge from the warmer forests below. As the seasons progress and the temperature begins to drop, they gradually migrate down the mountain, where they emerge from the forest in early morning and late afternoon.

The takin is Tangjiahe's flagship species and the easiest mammal to spot here. It uses regular tracks to move down to the river to drink; a strong musky odour from an oily substance that waterproofs its coat hits you when you reach the place where it crosses the road from the forest. Hunting, loss of habitat, road construction and disturbance from tourism have all contributed to a reduction in takin populations.

Five distinct vegetation bands occur at Tangjiahe. The lowest is the evergreen broad-leaved forest; this gives way to evergreen and deciduous forest, then to mixed coniferous and deciduous broad-leaved forest, subalpine coniferous forest and finally alpine meadow. At the lower levels, the first week in November is the prime time for the fiery autumn colours, but when we climbed up to 2,229 m (7,310 ft) to the Gansu border, the colours were spectacular. At this altitude, colder nights accelerate the breakdown of green chlorophyll in the leaves, so autumn peaks earlier.

^ The glory flower (*Clerodendrum bungei*) is a deciduous shrub with large heart-shaped leaves. After the fragrant pink flower clusters fade, gaudy turquoise/dark blue fruits, each with an enlarged red skirt-like calyx, attract the birds.

> Brambles belong to the genus *Rubus*, with many producing red or black berries made up of numerous single-seeded fruits called achenes. This one has particularly striking edible orange fruits and is just one of 54 species that occur in Sichuan.

< A red-billed blue magpie (*Urocissa erythrorhyncha*) pauses on a roof, clutching two Chinese gooseberries in its bill.

∨ In autumn, discarded wild Chinese gooseberry fruits dropped by feeding squirrels and monkeys litter the ground beneath the vines, revealing green flesh with tiny brown seeds.

By October, flowers are thin on the ground, although the remnants of late-summer flowers such as buddleias and hydrangeas are still apparent. A few autumnal blooms enlivened the bank sides as we passed; most conspicuously, a yellow-flowered composite resembling a miniature chrysanthemum was so abundant on open rock faces that from a distance it looked as if there were golden cascades flowing down from the rocky ledges. Beside the wider tracks I spotted the occasional erect pink single flower of what is known in British gardens as the Japanese anemone (*Anemone hupehensis* var. *japonica*), although it originates in China and has been naturalised in Japan for some time. The Scottish botanist Robert Fortune (1812–80) first introduced this lovely late-flowering perennial to English gardens in 1844, having spotted it 'in full bloom amongst the graves of the natives which are around the ramparts of Shanghai…'

Autumn is the season when the lower forests at Tangjiahe are enlivened with a colourful array of fruits on shrubs and trees. Red and orange fruits stand out amongst green foliage, helping to lure birds and mammals which distribute the seeds away from the parent plant, either by collecting them to eat elsewhere or by passing them through their droppings. No fewer than 35 species of wild roses grow here and the most robust ones with dense flower clusters produce copious bright red bunches of hips, festooning many a tree like Christmas baubles. It is impossible to walk for any length of time with your neck craned skywards in search of autumnal fruits; instead I keep an eye on the ground for fallen ones – intact or eaten – pinpointing the position of ripe berries on branches or vines above.

Robert Fortune also introduced the climbing Chinese gooseberry (*Actinidia chinensis*), better known outside China as kiwi fruit – thanks to an inspired marketing campaign by New Zealand growers. The brown fruits of the wild plant resemble miniature versions of the cultivated kiwi, hanging down from vines that scramble up and over trees; monkeys, squirrels, bears and larger birds all feast on them.

Finding mammals in densely forested mountain areas is a totally different experience from going on safari to Africa, driving in vehicles across vast open plains. Knowing the habits and favoured feeding or drinking places of some species certainly helps, but with most animals being thin on the ground at Tangjiahe, a considerable amount of legwork – not to mention a great deal of luck – has to go into tracking them. The reward therefore seems all the greater when you achieve a close encounter.

17

< A cluster of dead leaves inside the branches easily pinpoints the feeding platform of an Asian black bear in the fork of a tree. Bears make these platforms by bending down branches after stripping off the fruit.

> A captive Asian or Tibetan black bear shows how the long fur around its shoulders and neck resembles a mane. The distinctive white patch on the chest gives rise to the alternative name of moon bear.

ᵛ A male Reeves's muntjac moves through the forest to feed. The first Chinese muntjac came to England in the 1830s. They were kept in Woburn Park in Bedfordshire, from where they escaped, and have since spread over much of south and central England and into Wales.

^ The spiky husks of sweet chestnut fruit open to reveal the brown edible nuts inside. A week later, in Yangshuo, we ate a delicious stir-fry dish lavished with sweet chestnuts and cooked by the wife of a local guide.

I was fortunate to have three excellent trackers – in addition to Zorro, there were two local guides: Li Ying, who works at Tangjiahe specialising in birds, and Mr Yang, who carried my camera gear. They were both superb at spotting Reeves's muntjacs (*Muntiacus reevesi*) in the forest across the river from the hotel, which we reached via two cable bridges. These connect with forest trails that peter out as you climb up higher; then you just take your own pioneering route up the natural slope. The muntjacs were difficult to photograph because either we spooked them or they wove their way in and out of trees as they fed. These small deer are about the size of a Labrador dog and have a shiny reddish coat. They live a largely solitary life, constantly on the alert for predators. Both sexes have a prominent scent gland below each eye, used for scent marking, while the buck's upper canines extend backwards outside the lips like miniature tusks and are used for fighting other males. When alarmed, and during the rut, the male produces a loud barking sound, giving rise to the alternative name of barking deer.

These muntjacs are named after John Reeves (1774–1856), a taster for the East India Tea Company, who lived in China between 1812 and 1831. A keen amateur naturalist, he collected many specimens, including the Reeves's pheasant (*Syrmaticus reevesii*), and commissioned Chinese artists to make detailed botanical drawings in the Western style. As a result, more than 2,000 watercolours of plants and animals, including birds, mammals, reptiles, fishes, crustaceans, insects and shells, formed the first large collection of Chinese natural-history artwork to appear in the West.

The American zoologist George Schaller, together with Chinese scientists, has studied giant pandas extensively at Wolong since the 1980s. He used Tangjiahe as a study area for comparing the feeding patterns of pandas with those of Asian black bears (*Ursus thibetanus*). This research revealed that the bears have three distinct feeding periods during the year. After four months in hibernation, they emerge from their den between the end of March and mid-April to feed on the shoots and leaves of herbaceous plants and shrubs until mid-July. As the temperature rises, they move up the mountain to forage. Ripening fruits expand their diet until mid-September, when they move down again to feed on the acorns of several species of evergreen oaks (*Quercus* spp. and *Cyclobalanopsis oxyodon*), plus hazelnuts (*Corylus* spp.) and Manchurian walnuts (*Juglans mandshurica*). Acorns are an important food source as the bears build up their reserves before they hibernate again.

The sound of oak branches snapping as bears break them to gain access to acorns is one way of homing in on them. When feeding in the fork of a tree, a bear will pull in branches to enable it to reach the acorns; once these have been harvested, instead of letting the branches go, it pushes them beneath its feet to make a rough platform. Old feeding platforms are easily identified by the untidy mass of branches with dead leaves in the centre of a living tree.

19

^ A spotted nutcracker (*Nucifraga caryocatactes*) uses its powerful bill to prise open a Chinese red pine (*Pinus tabuliformis*) cone to feed on the seeds. Cones that these nutcrackers have previously worked remain on an upper branch.

> During the courtship display a male golden pheasant spreads his gold- and black-barred nape ruff like a miniature cape to attract the drab-coloured female.

↲ A green Chinese red pine cone shows scales prised open by a spotted nutcracker to extract the seeds.

The Tangjiahe bears also feed on Chinese gooseberries and the sweet red globose fruits of Chinese dogwood (*Cornus kousa chinensis*) that dangle from long stalks. Local people collect these fruits for wine making. Sadly, the closest I came to bears was finding recent scratch marks on a trunk and their droppings, with fruit remains much in evidence.

Wild boar (*Sus scrofa*) and squirrels feast on chestnuts as well as acorns. Père David's rock squirrels (*Sciurotamias davidianus*) are everywhere, bounding over rocks and up and down tree trunks and lianas. They have dark fur above and an attractive cream-coloured belly. While attempting to catch up with some squirrels with Mr Yang, I heard leaves rustling on the ground and assumed one of my group had walked round in a loop. Moments later we were confronted with a male boar foraging for acorns, quite oblivious to our presence. Once it detected our scent, it stopped dead in its tracks and was so tightly framed that I had to speedily reduce the focal length of my zoom lens. After we regrouped, Zorro said he had been very nervous about my safety and almost rushed across in my defence. I was glad he had restrained himself, as I would have missed the best wild boar shots of the trip!

China has a rich pheasant fauna, with 27 of the world's 50 species, most of which live in forests. One day we set off in high hopes of finding the glorious male golden pheasant (*Chrysolophus pictus*) by walking the track that follows the Bei Lu River uphill from the hotel. On the way we passed three researchers who were returning from a six-day hike into the heart of the mountains to collect giant panda droppings, which they do every season to determine how its diet changes. They told me the Tangjiahe giant panda population is around 60 individuals; no corpses had been found after the 2008 earthquake, but one agitated panda walked all the way down to the local town. The red or lesser panda (*Ailurus fulgens*) also occurs here, as do several cats, including lynx (*Lynx lynx*), leopard (*Panthera pardus*) and the striking clouded leopard (*Neofelis nebulosa*).

ᵛ A wild boar freezes as it looks up from feeding to see two people at close range.

Mr Yang and I made a detour off the track in what turned out to be a fruitless search for golden pheasants amongst bamboo clumps and bramble bushes. We returned to find Zorro beaming from ear to ear and holding his mobile phone to show us a video he had taken of a Chinese goral (*Nemorhaedus griseus*) emerging from the river and walking past him along the track.

Up to this point, apart from tadpoles in a pool, a black 'iron worm' which lives as a parasite inside mantids, takin and hog badger (a porcupine) footprints, it had been a poor day for wildlife watching. Then, thanks to Zorro, events changed very rapidly. We were looking at a snake when he spotted a goral in a cave up a cliff across the river. The events which followed were the most riveting in the whole trip, although, checking

^ Himalayan blue sheep (*Pseudois nayaur*) occur in Tangjiahe and other parts of Sichuan, as well as in the montane regions of the Himalayas. When threatened, they freeze and blend in with their surroundings, but they are also able to race up precipitous cliffs with great agility.

ˇ Beside an abandoned house in Tangjiahe used as a shelter by takin, the walls of an old cooker fuelled by wood have been colonised by mosses and liverworts.

> A photo sequence shows how a Chinese goral moved from a cave entrance high up a sheer rock face down to the Bei Lu River below. Judging by the worn tracks on the rocks, this tortuous path had been used on a regular basis over many years.

the times on my digital images later, I found that they were all over in 16 seconds. The description of the goral's descent appears in the opening paragraph of this chapter. All too rarely with wildlife do you get the opportunity of a repeat performance, but within minutes the goral took precisely the same route again.

Despite its name, the Chinese goral is not confined to China, but occurs through Burma, India, Thailand, Vietnam and possibly Laos. It lives in the high mountain ranges, including the Himalayas, especially along sparsely vegetated cliffs with small crevices where it can hide. Small, almost vertical toes provide a good grip on steep rocky slopes and make it extremely agile. The goral has very few natural enemies, because its habitat is so inhospitable to other animals.

Before leaving Britain, I was optimistic of spotting the Tibetan macaque (*Macaca thibetana*), the largest macaque in the world, and we missed a sighting by minutes after a road worker told us he had seen macaques feeding on ripe persimmon fruit on his way into the reserve. By the time we arrived at the scene they had vanished.

So I headed south of Chengdu to Emeishan (*aka* Mount Omei*) to see the Tibetan macaques. My last visit to this mountain had been in 1984, with a group of rhododendron enthusiasts from New Zealand. In those days, we had to walk up countless steps to reach the 3,099 m (10,170 ft) summit. One of the four Buddhist sacred mountains in China, Emeishan was designated a UNESCO World Heritage Site in 1996, primarily for its cultural significance, for it is here that Buddhism first became established in China. Also an area of natural beauty with a great diversity of plant species, it has attracted plantsmen ever since E. H. Wilson first visited it in 1903. Yet, compared to many Chinese mountains, Emeishan is unimpressive and far too low to retain any snow at the top.

This mountain lures crowds of day tourists from Chengdu, their ascent now eased by two cable cars. We spent the night in a hotel near one of these, so that we could take an early ride up to the Wannian Monastery and then walk down to the monkey-watching area before the tours arrived. After we had waited for over an hour and a half, a cry went out as a troop was located 500 m (1,600 ft) along the path. By this time, the number of visitors was steadily increasing. I prefer to stand back and use a long lens, so that I can photograph several different monkeys simply by changing the camera angle, but this proved hopeless. With virtually everyone taking pictures at close range using point-and-shoot cameras or mobile phones, every way

I turned there was a sea of heads. I wandered up the path in front of the crowd, only to be thwarted by a monkey warden with a stick blocking the path for 'my safety'. Having taken the precaution of emptying all traces of food from my pockets, I was confident I was at a much lower risk of attack than the Chinese tourists clutching plastic lunch bags.

Then the strategy became all too evident. The wardens were scattering maize grain to entice the monkeys down the path to the area where commercial photographers persuaded visitors to have their picture taken alongside them. By not following the mob, I was delaying the monkeys' descent. How much better it would have been for the wild monkeys to be provisioned with food in a regular feeding area – as they are in Monkey Valley at the base of Huangshan – instead of this carrot-and-stick approach.

Despite this disappointment, I had seen another macaque species. Fortunately, Tangjiahe is much more remote than Emeishan and although the new road will inevitably bring more tourists, the scientists working there will no doubt monitor the effect this may have on the wildlife – especially the mammals.

Tangjiahe is a glorious place to visit at any time of year. Wild flowers abound in spring, when Chinese redbud trees (*Cercis chinensis*) are bursting into bloom; in summer the takin congregate in the alpine meadows; autumn brings vibrant colour to the forests, while winter snow adds its own ephemeral beauty to this enchanting reserve.

<< Like the giant panda, red pandas are active in winter. This one descended from a tree to forage on bamboo in snow at Wolong, further south in Sichuan.

< A young Tibetan or Père David's macaque nuzzles up against its mother as it plays with a branch on Emeishan, where 1.21 million visitors converged in 2008.

^ Tibetan macaques have an obvious beard and well developed cheek whiskers that frame the hairless face, which appears much redder in females than in males.

CHAPTER 2

THE BAMBOO SEA

An overview of temperate woodland or tropical rainforest shows rounded crowns forming the canopy mosaic; not so a bird's-eye view of a verdant bamboo forest. From the top of a peak or a cable car, this resembles a green sea, with the bowed bamboo tips rippling in the breeze like waves. Small wonder the Chinese people refer to the area as Shunan Zhuhai or the Bamboo Sea. From above, this primeval forest appears to be essentially a uniform carpet of bamboo yet, once you step inside, the range of bamboo types becomes apparent. In amongst the bamboos, covering peaks, ridges and hills, is a rich assortment of plants – from mosses and ferns to shrubs and woody trees – creating a diverse habitat that supports a host of animal life.

< A view up inside a moso bamboo (*Phyllostachys pubescens*) canopy shows the culms reaching for the sky within the South Sichuan Bamboo Forest National Park. In spring, the new shoots of this bamboo can grow as much as 30–48 cm (12–19 in) in a single day and reach their full height in 40–50 days, but it takes five years for the culms to mature.

27

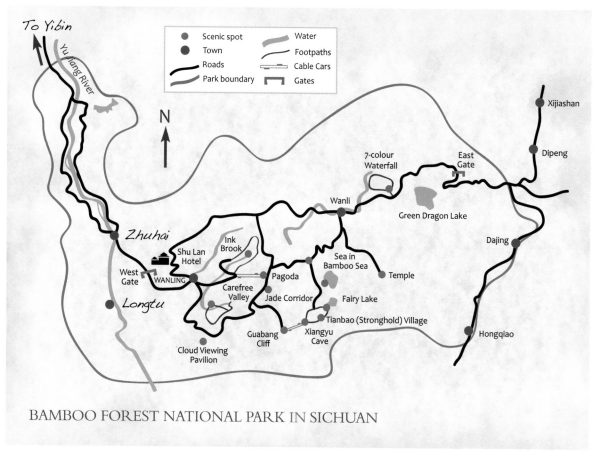

To Yibin

Yu Jiang River

Scenic spot | **Water**
Town | **Footpaths**
Roads | **Cable Cars**
Park boundary | **Gates**

N

Xijiashan

Dipeng

7-colour Waterfall

East Gate

Wanli

Green Dragon Lake

Zhuhai

Dajing

Ink Brook

Shu Lan Hotel

Sea in Bamboo Sea

Temple

West Gate

WANLING

Pagoda

Carefree Valley

Jade Corridor

Fairy Lake

Longtu

Guabang Cliff

Xiangyu Cave

Tianbao (Stronghold) Village

Hongqiao

Cloud Viewing Pavilion

BAMBOO FOREST NATIONAL PARK IN SICHUAN

Having made a fleeting visit to the South Sichuan Bamboo Sea in April, a couple of years before, I had seen enough to give me the impetus to return. In addition, *Chinese National Geography* magazine rated it as one of the ten most beautiful forests in China, punctuated by lakes, rivers and waterfalls. The timing for most of my trips to China is determined by seasonal considerations such as the optimum time for breeding birds, alpine flowers or autumn tints. With bamboo, this wasn't so much of an issue, but the only time I had a week to spare was in late August. This was during the peak summer-holiday season for the Chinese, so the forest was going to be busier than I would have liked, but I had no alternative. It would also be much hotter than during my previous visit, but at an altitude of 600–1000 m (2,000–3,300 ft) the area is, for the most part, warm in winter, cool in summer, so it is a congenial place all year round.

The South Sichuan Bamboo Sea, which officially became the Bamboo Forest National Park in 1988,

lies 300 km (185 miles) south of Chengdu, with a driving time optimistically quoted as five hours. It took us nearer six, passing through Yibin. Yibin is the nearest city to the Bamboo Sea and is known as the first city on the upper reaches of the Yangtze, although it actually lies on the Yujiang, which flows into the larger river. We entered the park via the West Gate and just managed to squeeze into the last available gap in the hotel car park. Featured in the Oscar-winning film *Crouching Tiger, Hidden Dragon*, the Bamboo Sea attracts increasing numbers of Chinese tourists, many of whom travel by bus from Chengdu or Chongqing.

> Overview of the Bamboo Sea from the cable car, showing hardwood trees dotted amongst the bamboo. Huang Tingjian, a poet in the Northern Song Dynasty, was so impressed by the scene that he commented, 'The waves of the bamboo spread to thousands of miles, which inebriates me like good wine.'

^ The attractive Asiatic dayflower (*Commelina communis*) is an annual plant native to much of East Asia. The Chinese name *yazhicao* means 'duckfoot herb'. Asiatic dayflowers growing on copper mine spoils in eastern China accumulate very high concentrations of copper.

^ Policemen help clean up the flooded Shu Lan Hotel lobby after 182 mm (over 7 in) of rain fell during the night of 28/29 August 2009 – over one seventh of the area's mean annual rainfall. Red silt was carried down with the flood.

^ A crab crawls out onto red sandstone rock after the flood in the Bamboo Sea. These crustaceans fall prey to the crab-eating mongoose (*Herpestes urva*), which also feasts on fish, frogs, birds and reptiles.

> One of many waterfalls in Carefree Valley cascades over red sandstone rock, framed here with overhanging bamboos. The red rock with attached plants has been swept down by the flood.

That first night I awoke around midnight to hear heavy rain falling with thunder overhead. I rolled over, musing that the raised humidity would create a sea of clouds above the bamboo forest once the temperature rose. However, by 6.30 a.m. a commotion downstairs, punctuated by resonating loud cracks from bamboo stems breaking, aroused my curiosity enough to make me draw back the curtains. Below, I saw a red river racing down the path towards the lobby in the main building and hotel staff wading through it. Dressing rapidly, I waded through a moon gate before the water cascaded down steps into the lobby, where staff and guests were standing around in disbelief. With power lines down and a flooded dining-room, it was no surprise breakfast was off. Fortunately, I always carry emergency rations of rice crackers, soft drinks and dull pink candies made from outsized *shanzha* (Chinese hawthorn, *Crataegus pinnatifida*) fruits.

By now the rain was beginning to abate and, as staff emerged clutching handfuls of pristine brooms, I nipped back to my room for a camera and took some surreal shots of staff and policemen sweeping the flood water out through the doors of the lobby. The Bamboo Sea lies on red sandstone and the water carried the red silt everywhere it flowed – inside buildings and down roads. This was later removed using shovels and high-pressure hoses. Freshwater and land crabs were flushed out onto tracks and roads, where many ended up as road kills.

My guide, Jing Zhong (known as Zorro), my driver, Mr Zhou, and I walked down the road to gauge the situation and found it blocked with fallen bamboo culms. Fortunately, bamboo being a giant grass with a hollow stem, it is much speedier to chop through than solid woody tree trunks. The police stopped all cars going down to the West Gate, but most bikers ignored their warnings and set off through the flood water. Mr Zhou decided to try to drive uphill to Wangyou or Carefree Valley. Here is a stunning blend of bamboo groves, countless winding streams and precipitous waterfalls, although not everyone reaches the highest fall via stepped paths with increasingly high risers.

^ Growing in wet forests, the spinulose tree fern has suffered from the selective felling of large trees that can no longer cast shade – even more crucial as the climate becomes drier – and from over-collection. The stem, known as *longgufeng* (dragon bone stem), has long been used in Traditional Chinese Medicine to strengthen joints. More recently, the plant has become a much prized ornamental plant in gardens.

∨ A sodden cricket with outsized antennae crawls up onto a moso bamboo culm to dry out after the storm.

^ As a hornet raids brood in a wasp nest, the wasps take avoiding action by clustering at the top of the nest. Many kinds of hornet occur in China and the adults of some species are soaked in spirits for use in TCM, while the brood is considered a local delicacy in the neighbouring province of Yunnan.

∨ In Carefree Valley, wasps are busily adding *papier-mâché* to their paper nest attached to a bamboo stem and attending to their brood.

Mosses, ferns and selaginellas flourish on the shady banks. As we passed, a host of invertebrates – crickets, grasshoppers, caterpillars, moths, butterflies, flies and spiders – began to emerge from where they had found shelter during the deluge. Large black swallowtail butterflies seemed to be perpetually on the wing as they circumnavigated their territory, powering their way to the tops of waterfalls and down again, barely pausing on the way.

Two special plants, now rarely seen in the forest, are the spinulose tree fern (*Cyathea spinulosa*) and a cycad (*Cycas revoluta*), also known as sago palm, although it is unrelated to palms. Cycads and tree ferns have a long lineage and are both regarded as living fossils. *Cycas revoluta* produces separate male and female plants that rely on both wind and insects to spread the pollen from the male to the female cone.

Zorro found an elongated wasp nest attached to a bamboo stem, constructed by wasps sporting spectacular red heads, yellow eyes and black and white striped abdomens. The light was so poor I had no option but to use flash to freeze their movements, praying as I did so this would not induce them to dive-bomb me. In fact, it had the reverse effect; all the wasps froze on the nest. Spotting them was a lucky bonus. Then, just as I was packing up, a huge hornet landed, causing the wasps to congregate towards the top of the nest, while the hornet raided the brood within their cells in the base.

ᵛ A praying mantid (*Mantis religiosa*) casts a shadow as it walks over a path in Carefree Valley late in the day. The spiny forelegs used for snaring prey are evident from the shadow.

^ Late in the day, an orange oakleaf or dead leaf butterfly (*Kallima inachus*) rests on a fern in Carefree Valley. Open wings reveal bright colours above, whereas the underwings resemble a withered leaf – complete with false veins and even insect damage. This famous mimicry insect is widely sought after by butterfly collectors.

Late afternoon in Carefree Valley produced several choice insects. Among green foliage green praying mantids are masters of disguise, but two gravid females were conspicuous on the red sandstone path. I could not believe my luck when an orange oak leaf or dead leaf butterfly alighted on a fern right beside where I was standing, allowing me to photograph the colourful open wings and also the camouflaged underwings. In shape and colour these resemble a dry brown leaf, complete with leaf veins, and they even have markings that mimic insect damage (see page 131).

Throughout the day, black-winged damselflies flit across streams, but their full glory is revealed only late

< A male damselfly finds a sunny patch on a path, where he displays to attract a female by flashing the blue iridescent spots inside his wings.

in the day, when they alight in a patch of sunlight. Then their iridescent turquoise bodies and green heads glow jewel-like against the black wings. However, the *coup de grâce* comes when the wings open out to flash a deep blue iridescent patch inside each one.

Emerging from the leaf litter above the flood-water level were several *Mabuya* skinks – lizards with smooth, scaled skins and diminutive legs. They spend most of the time on the ground amongst the leaf litter, typically basking in a sunspot beamed down from the canopy or along a riverbank. One took an optimistic lunge at a medium-sized crab, which rapidly scuttled away.

In the forest at night I listened in vain for the call of the famed xylophone or harpist frog, which is green and white above with a pink belly. The call is a warbling, melodious song that resembles a xylophone.

Throughout the Bamboo Forest there are vantage points for viewing scenic spots. One of these is an eight-storey pagoda at the top of the cable car and

^ Framed by a lattice window from inside the pavilion in Xianyu (Celestial Dwelling) Cave is a sea of clouds above the Bamboo Forest.

another the Cloud Viewing Pavilion. The vegetation has now grown so tall that it completely blocks the view from the pavilion itself, but a flat area below it overlooks a plethora of small hills, with the distant mountains marking the transition between the Sichuan Basin and the Yungui Plateau. One of the scenic views displayed during the opening ceremony of the 2008 Beijing Olympics was taken here. It depicts hills emerging from a cloud base, looking for all the world like a multitude of turtle shells. Each morning I rose early in the hope of seeing this ephemeral view and drove out with my long-suffering driver and guide, only to find a blanket cloud cover. Later I learnt that the photographer who took the Olympics image spent a month here before achieving his striking result.

35

Virtually all the Chinese tourists departed rapidly on the day of the flood. Certainly the high heels I had spotted on one guest were ill-suited for a stroll in the forest in normal conditions, let alone after a deluge. The hotel had been fully booked but after the first night I was the sole visitor left. The extent of the damage (numerous landslides of red earth had been dumped on roads and others had become unsafe because of undercutting) was quickly assessed and a decision was made to close the Bamboo Sea to all new tourists. Apart from local residents, suddenly Zorro and I had the park almost to ourselves. A few places were out of bounds for safety reasons and the cable car was not running, but fortunately I had been up on my first visit. Each day I expected the police to ask us to leave, but miraculously we were allowed to stay and to travel where we chose.

The main disadvantage of the flood was being without electricity for two days. This meant I could not charge my camera batteries or my laptop. At night the hotel provided candles and I had my wind-up torch. For washing and drinking we were back in the 1980s, when every hotel room was supplied night and morning with a huge thermos of boiled water. Restaurants dependent on electricity closed their shutters, but we found a farmer's house with a wood stove, where we returned for all our meals – with vegetables plucked from the garden after we arrived.

The Administrative Bureau Office of the national park is located at the West Gate. Once a huge landslip had been cleared from the road, I was eager to visit to get information about the area, because all I had managed to glean so far was a leaflet extracted from beneath a pile of tourist knick-knacks in a glass cabinet at the park entrance. After I had produced my business card, a very helpful lady found several more brochures and a DVD – all with limited English text, but useful for checking against my target list of species. Clutching a goodies bag, I emerged to find my driver talking to a Sichuan Television crew. They were desperate to interview someone about their flood experiences and since they could not pass through the entrance gate and no visitors had emerged all the time they were there, they pounced on me. I was looking forward to speaking enthusiastically about why I was here and what I had seen, but they only wanted me to answer two questions. 'Was I scared about the flood?', to which I replied 'No, it was a big adventure', and 'Did I have enough food to eat?' 'Yes, because there were so few people left to eat it.'

> Sun beams down onto bamboo leaves at the end of the day.

Gradually, depressing news from further afield began to filter through. In the nearby town of Longtu, through which the Yujiang flows, seven people had died in the flood and two were missing. During that single night 182 mm (over 7 in) of rain had fallen in the Bamboo Forest area – more than one seventh of the average annual rainfall in this subtropical humid monsoon zone. As we explored new areas we repeatedly saw huge bamboos uprooted, colossal rocks dumped downstream and one impressive waterfall reduced to a mere trickle after the blocked stream had rerouted itself.

Bamboo dominates the forest. The most impressive is moso bamboo – the fastest-growing plant in the world – which can grow up to 24 m (78 ft) high in under two months. It has for long been utilised in many practical as well as aesthetic ways: not only can bamboo be eaten, it is also invaluable in building and can even be made into fabrics and household items such as teapots. Being fast-

^ Wang Shi Huai, aged 84, smokes a pipe made from a slender bamboo stem with copper ends. Quite coincidentally, the exhaled smoke resembles a face in profile.

< Bamboos line the Jade Corridor, a famous scenic road in the Bamboo Sea which is always cool even in summer.

growing it is easily sustainable as well as being biodegradable. The stems or culms are cut selectively in rotation, the largest being used for building houses and smaller ones providing handrails for pedestrian bridges across streams. Some old bamboo products, including a sedan chair, are displayed in the Bamboo Sea Museum – the only one in China to specialise in bamboo.

Most local dishes contain bamboo shoots, which are eaten raw, steamed, boiled or stir-fried. Such dishes are often served wrapped in bamboo leaves or inside a

sectioned bamboo stem. A special delicacy of the region is the bamboo fungus or veiled lady (*Phallus indusiatus*), known by the Chinese name *zhu sheng*. This is a type of stinkhorn fungus with an attractive lacy veil around the white stem bearing a mass of spores on top. The subterranean egg stage and the fully developed fungus are eaten both fresh and from rehydrated dried specimens out of season. As it is high in protein and low in fat, its many benefits are said to include a general health improvement and weight loss. Fungus gatherers jealously guard their productive patches and, as demand has grown, this is one of many edible fungi now cultivated in China. On exposure to air, the spore mass produces a pungent smell that attracts flies to walk over the spores as they feed. They then inadvertently carry the spores on their bodies and thereby help to disperse the fungus.

39

^ The female great mormon (*Papilio memnon*) is one of many
swallowtails that visit wild hydrangea flowers to feed. They belong
to the Papilionidae family and the females of this species have many
different tail forms. When the large butterflies feed, fragments
of the blue stamens rain down on the leaves below.

< Wild *Hydrangea aspera* flowers provide a vital late-summer food
source for many insects in the Bamboo Sea.

I despaired of getting close to the ever–mobile
large black swallowtail butterflies, until we rounded a
corner of a road to see several lift off from flat-topped
Hydrangea aspera flowers. The plant was rooted in a gully
several metres below the road, with many flowers more
or less at my eye level – perfect for observing and
photographing the insects.

^ When a common bluebottle butterfly (*Graphium sarpedon*) feeds on hydrangea flowers, the wings constantly vibrate as they are held vertically – ready to make a hasty retreat. This swallowtail seeks out the highest flowers and has much briefer feeding spells than the larger swallowtails. The larvae feed on cinnamon leaves and other members of the laurel family.

The flattened flower heads were large enough for several insects to dine at the same table – butterflies, moths, wasps and an outsized bee were all feasting on this attractive shrub. Even so, there was a distinct hierarchy, with the largest insects not always calling the tune. A black and white butterfly – half the size of the large swallowtails – not only saw off any that attempted to land, but also made periodic sorties to check out swallowtails feeding elsewhere, seeking to dislodge them. This male great eggfly (*Hypolimnas bolina*) is notorious for being highly territorial. Virtually all the swallowtails showed some wing damage from predators attacking their trailing tails. Most flew actively from one flower to another, although one floated gracefully, barely flapping its wings. Mantids, dragonflies, frogs, lizards and birds all feed on these butterflies, targeting them sipping on nectar or drinking at puddles. As the butterfly takes off, the predator attacks the showy tail, leaving the head and thorax intact.

^ Two images of the same male great eggfly feeding on a wild *Hydrangea aspera* flower. The blue iridescent areas appear around the two largest white spots on each wing only when seen from the front and lit by sun or by flash on the camera. Eggflies are a group of butterflies known for the marked differences between males and females.

^ A water drop forms on an *Impatiens* flower as water runs off a sheer rock in the Bamboo Sea.

< Storm damage in Black Brook Valley shows where the red earth has collapsed, taking many bamboos down with it.

The Dragon Sea and the Seven Colours Waterfall are repeatedly written up as two key spots in the Bamboo Sea, but after the flood had caused a building to collapse into the Dragon Sea lake, this area was closed and little water was flowing over the nearby waterfall.

However, not all was lost, because beside the path overlooking the fall, a shady rock face dripping with water had extensive patches of *Impatiens* at the base. Further along the path, an even wetter rock face provided perfect conditions for the delicate membranous fronds of a maidenhair fern (*Adiantum* spp.) to flourish alongside liverworts and selaginellas.

Mr Zhou volunteered to carry my photo pack down the precipitous steps to the ancient cliff road known as the Celestial Dwelling Cave, cut into a red sandstone cliff, but had to turn back when he began to suffer from vertigo. This walk is certainly not for the faint hearted, with steep ravines falling away beneath the track. The reward, however, is the most spectacular view in the Bamboo Sea – across a deep valley to a red rock face with another cliff walkway cut into it. The rock passageway runs beneath an overhanging cliff, passing a pavilion that overlooks the Sea of Clouds and a Taoist guardian painted onto the rock. The original Buddhist temple later became a Taoist one. Just before a narrow waterfall drops into a plunge pool, a giant sleeping Buddha was carved into the rock as recently as 1993.

The flood damage was so severe in Black Brook Valley that we managed to gain access only on our last day and even then we saw no other visitors. The stream, also known as Ink Creek, is named from the legend which says that when Huang Tingjian, a poet of the Northern Song Dynasty (AD 960–1127), visited the creek he wrote, 'I am drunk with the beautiful scenery' and threw his ink brush into the water, creating its sombre colour. In this valley, large bamboos had been completely uprooted as a result of the storm. Butterflies clustered beside the path to feed on minerals, and lifted off in a fluttering flight as we passed them. Just below a waterfall, large rocks brought down by the swollen stream had broken up the stone path. There was no way that a heavy vehicle could reach this part of the Bamboo Sea, so all the repairs would have to be done by hand. We heard that the estimate for the flood damage was 300 million RMB (£26.5 million).

During my brief spell in the Bamboo Sea I was fortunate to glean some insight to the diverse life that inhabits this unique forest, one I feel privileged to have explored virtually on my own. I long to return in winter when snow transforms the verdant vistas!

∨ This red sandstone cliff with its pavilion and the site of the Taoist temple in Celestial Dwelling Cave is a provincial protected cultural site.

CHAPTER 3

LIFE-GIVING WATER

It was one of those idyllic afternoons. Waves were breaking on the shore as strings of cormorants and gulls streamed past the cliff top against a clear blue sky with a skylark singing overhead. Nothing extraordinary here – it could have been a cliff top along any coastline where seabirds congregate to nest; except that I was more than 1,600 km (1,000 miles) from the coast at 3,196 m (10,486 ft) above sea level. China's largest inland lake lies within Qinghai Province on the north-east of the Qinghai-Tibetan Plateau. Flanked on all four sides by mountains, Qinghai Hu is so vast it could easily be mistaken for a sea; indeed in ancient times it was known as the West Sea.

< Clear, sunny days transform the water of China's largest inland salt-water lake from a drab grey to varying shades of blue or green. Annual lake-worshipping ceremonies for Qinghai Hu were originally a Mongolian tradition, but have now become a Tibetan one: sacrifices are offered to the lake during the Tibetan New Year.

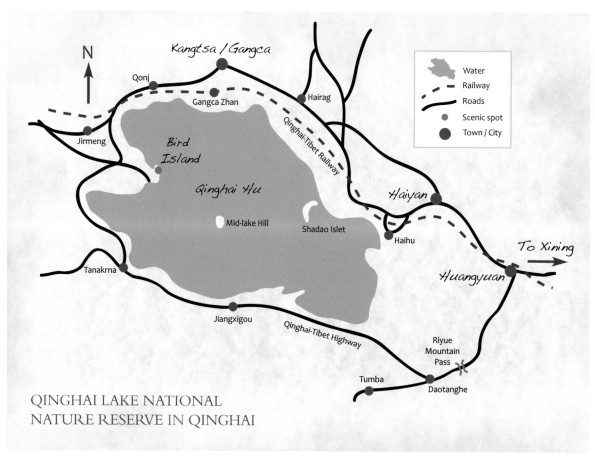

Kangtsa / Gangca

Qonj

Gangca Zhan

Hairag

Jirmeng

Bird
Island

Qinghai-Tibet Railway

Qinghai Hu

Haiyan

Mid-lake Hill

Shadao Islet

Haihu

To Xining

Tanakrna

Huangyuan

Jiangxigou

Qinghai-Tibet Highway

Riyue
Mountain
Pass

Tumba

Daotanghe

	Water
	Railway
	Roads
	Scenic spot
	Town / City

QINGHAI LAKE NATIONAL
NATURE RESERVE IN QINGHAI

Qinghai Hu, sometimes referred to by its older Mongolian name of Koko Nor, lies at the crossroads of several bird migration routes across Asia. It is an important breeding site for many species attracted by the fish, including the once-abundant naked carp (*Gymnocypris przewalskii*) which was enjoyed by people as well as birds.

Chinese National Geography ranks Qinghai as one of the five most beautiful lakes in China; but however much you research a location you can never be sure it will meet your expectations. On the plus side, I knew that any wetland with ample nesting sites and copious food supplies could attract large numbers of colonial nesting birds. But I also knew that a severe outbreak of Avian flu H5N1 virus in 2005 had killed tens of thousands of wild birds and resulted in the lake being closed.

May and June are the best months for bird-watching at Qinghai, so I arranged a trip in mid-May and requested a bird expert as my guide. Jia Min, who arranged the tour for me, managed to find an expert but warned me that he had minimal English. Indeed, when Mr Rong Guo Cheng

↗ Brown-headed gulls hover above Qinghai Lake NNR, the black-tipped primary wing feathers with conspicuous white mirrors clearly visible on one bird. Niaodao, or Bird Island, a rocky peninsula that juts out into the lake, was declared a Ramsar site in 1992.

> Courting brown-headed gulls on Qinghai Hu (*hu* is the Chinese for lake). In the winter, when the lake freezes, herbivorous species including several types of duck, goose and swan overwinter here.

>> The red ring of bare skin surrounding the eye and the outer white eye crescents are clearly visible in this portrait of a brown-headed gull.

met me at Xining airport, he was clutching a Chinese-English dictionary and clearly taking his task very seriously. He presented me with an attractive booklet introducing Qinghai Lake NNR; it was copiously illustrated with colour photographs and boasted both Chinese and English text. He also had a copy of the Chinese edition of the *Field Guide to Chinese Birds*. This boded well.

Xining, the capital city of Qinghai Province, has a history dating back 2,100 years; it used to be the only gateway to the Tangbo Ancient Road and Silk Road. At an altitude of 2,261m (7,418 ft), it is neither too cold in winter nor too hot in summer. Qinghai Hu lies to the west of Xining, from where it takes just an hour and a half via an expressway to reach the eastern shore.

A quick word from Mr Rong to the barrier guard at the start of the 16 km (10 mile) long highway to Bird Island, a rocky peninsula that juts out into the lake, ensured we were waved through, proving that he was going to be a great asset. We then found our passage blocked by a gaggle of brown-headed gulls (*Larus brunicephalus*). Like many gulls, these are

< When a brown-headed gull calls, its red mouth becomes clearly visible. This migratory gull breeds on the Tibetan plateau and elsewhere in central Asia and then overwinters on coasts and large inland lakes within tropical southern Asia.

opportunist feeders, gathering wherever people congregate in the hope of a few titbits.

A new day revealed overcast skies plus a strong breeze at 6 a.m., so the wind-chill factor was considerable when we reached the cliff top overlooking Cormorant Rock. Only then could I begin to appreciate the vast size of Qinghai Hu. The water appeared to go on forever. The area used to be quoted as covering 5,694 km² (2,278 sq miles), but for the last half-century it has been shrinking. Before the 1960s over a hundred freshwater rivers fed into the lake; half of these have now dried up. Between 1959 and 1982 the water level dropped an average of 10 cm (4 in) annually, with overgrazing and land reclamation contributing to a reduction in the lake's surface area. For a while the levels then fluctuated, but since 2005 they have risen each year – due to high rainfall and global warming causing glaciers and snow around the lake margins to melt.

Pollution is another problem. To help restore the balance and protect this important wetland, the Qinghai Province government launched a ten-year project in 2008. The proposed measures include the removal of one million sheep, the reversion of pasture to grassland, the relocation of over 4,000 residents and a programme of tree-planting (hopefully of native rather than exotic species). Visitors to Bird Island will use a raised walkway skirting the lake.

^ Telltale white splashes of guano pinpoint the cliffs occupied by great cormorants (*Phalacrocorax carbo sinensis*), which build large, somewhat untidy nests from twigs.

< By April, great cormorants arrive to seek suitable nest sites on rocks and headlands on the north-west shore. Atop Cormorant Rock members of the colony build nests equally spaced from one another. At daybreak, cameos of life are apparent. While some birds are still asleep on their nests, others are stretching their wings, accepting nesting material from a mate or taking off to feed.

Egg Island, which rises less than 10 m (33 ft) above the water level, is where over 100,000 birds converge to nest – notably bar-headed geese (*Anser indicus*) and brown-headed gulls. Every spring, before the snow has completely melted, over 80 per cent of the world population of bar-headed geese make an impressive migration from India to Qinghai Hu to breed. Their route takes them over the Himalayas at an altitude of 9,000 m (30,000 ft) – a phenomenal feat that is achieved by concentrating more haemoglobin in the red blood cells than any other bird and using the jet stream to accelerate their passage.

The bird population on Egg Island is so dense that the ground becomes littered with goose eggs – hence the name. Like planes landing on a runway, all the geese flew in from the same direction, which meant that a couple of the windows in the island's huge hide were better than the rest for flight and landing shots. On the ground there was plenty of activity: if one goose showed an aggressive display by stretching and lowering its neck to hiss, neighbouring geese took evasive action, either running off a few paces or leaping up into the air. Periodically, something triggered a disturbance; then all the birds within one area became alert with up-stretched necks; some even took flight.

Many accounts of the lake emphasise the glorious and changing colours of the water; indeed, Qinghai and Koko Nor both mean Blue/Teal Sea. For the first couple of days of my visit, however, the overcast weather kept the water an unimpressive shade of grey. On the third day, we awoke to a sky with thin high cloud that soon cleared. As we climbed to a new cliff top, the lake was transformed into an electric blue colour.

∧ Viewed from inside the capacious hide, a continuous stream of bar-headed geese flies in at the edge of the breeding colony. One uses its wings to brake and then swerves to avoid landing on snoozing geese.

> Four bar-headed geese fly past their breeding ground. These geese begin to arrive when the lake is still frozen.

∨ A bar-headed goose walks in front of the hide, showing the distinct bars on its head.

> Great cormorants dry their wings and Pallas's gulls (*Larus ichthyaetus*) wait for a fish shoal to pass by a sand bar in Qinghai Hu.

While I was immersed in maximising the photo opportunities Mr Rong raced towards me, mobile phone in his outstretched hand. It was Jia Min, telling me that Mr Rong was concerned the electricity would be turned off in my hotel for 24 hours; but he had found another hotel with both electricity and an internet connection.

Reluctant to leave Bird Island, I lingered to savour the early evening light, so it was past 6 p.m. when we set off round the lake in a westerly direction. After an hour of driving, and well after darkness had fallen, we crested a hill to see a town below glowing with electric lights. On arrival at the Xuheng Holiday Hotel, I discovered that we had driven around half of Qinghai Hu to the eastern side. Mr Rong then produced the NNR brochure and pointed to pictures of Przewalski's gazelle (*Procapra przewalskii*) and black-necked cranes (*Grus nigricollis*). The reason for our long evening drive became clear – these were to be the objects of our quest the next day.

In the morning we made an early start to search for Przewalski's gazelle, named after the Russian scientist Nikolai Przewalski (1839–88), who first identified it in Inner Mongolia in 1875. Since the recent discovery of three new herds near the Qinghai Basin, the total world population is now 700–800 animals. Even so, this means the Przewalski's gazelle is rarer than the giant panda and I sensed it would be like looking for a needle in a haystack.

We picked up a local warden, ill dressed for the bitter wind – which felt as though it had originated from Siberia – in slip-on shoes and a leather jacket. After he and Mr Rong made a short exploration, gesticulating that they could not find any gazelles, we moved to a wetland area at Xiao Bo Hu for black-necked cranes. Using Mr Rong's binoculars, the warden soon found a crane and retreated to his house with Mr Rong for refreshments. With the bird a long way off and bending down to feed, I walked slowly forwards. Eventually it straightened itself and began to stride up a sand dune: rather incongruous for a wetland bird, but a fitting finale to my spell at Qinghai Hu.

My next wetland location would be much warmer, since it was farther south and was earmarked for the summer, when the lotus lilies would be in full bloom.

∧ Part of the vast breeding ground of bar-headed geese on Egg Island shows many scattered eggs.

∨ A Qinghai toad-headed lizard (*Phyrnocephalus vlangalii*) pauses on a sand dune. The disruptive coloration ensures it blends in with the sand when viewed from a distance.

53

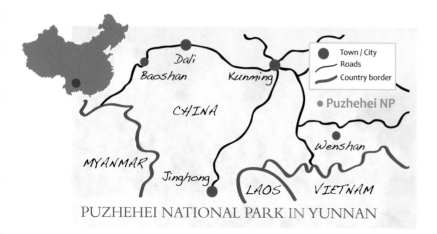

PUZHEHEI NATIONAL PARK IN YUNNAN

> Puzhehei National Park in south-east Yunnan is a mosaic of wetlands and peaks. The view from the Jade Dragon Peak shows some of the cultivated areas with rice paddies and lotus lilies. This landscape is peppered with lakes, mountains and caves, with emerald ribbon-like rivers weaving their way around the base of the forest-covered peaks.

Lotus lily flowers are exquisite at every stage of their development – from the bud bursting to the petals opening and then falling to reveal the flat-topped receptacle that carries the embedded seeds. Gliding through acres of blooming lotus on Puzhehei Hu in southern Yunnan, with dragonflies flitting past, is a heavenly way to travel, reminiscent of my *shikara* trip three decades ago on Kashmir's Dal Lake where the boatman used heart-shaped paddles. This time, the addition of karst peaks created a stunning three-dimensional landscape that should put Puzhehei high on the list of China's most beautiful lakes. The intimate and secret nature of small water bodies flowing around erupting peaks is infinitely more attractive than the vast Qinghai Hu.

54

<< Massed lotus lilies in flower; this aquatic plant soon invades shallow parts of calm open water in tropical and subtropical regions.

< Sacred lotus lily plants grow in mud at the bottom of water, producing statuesque buds that open after the leafless stalk grows up well above the surface. The beautiful flowers have long been associated with both Buddhism and Hinduism.

∨ A white lotus lily flower with pink-edged petals blooms in Puzhehei Hu. The lotus flower symbolises purity and divine birth. The copious pink as well as white blooms at Puzhehei are a huge attraction, culminating in a Lotus Festival in mid-July.

The name Puzhehei, derived from the language of the local Yi minority, means 'lake abundant with fish and shrimps'. Glimpses of these links in the aquatic food chain, together with waterweeds streaming just below the surface, can be had from the low-level boats. The area, which lies south-east of Kunming, was declared a national park in January 2009. It contains 300 karst peaks, 68 lakes and 73 karst caves. But the jewels in Puzhehei's crown are unquestionably the lotus lilies that bedeck the limpid waters in midsummer.

For the Yi people, the lotus is symbolic of their life-giving waters. At Puzhehei, it begins to bloom in June and continues throughout July and August, with the annual Lotus Festival being held in mid-July. Flower production coincides with the wet season, when the weather can change rapidly from a glorious sunny day to a torrential downpour. This combination makes for hot and very humid conditions when the sun is shining.

The best overview of the area is gained by climbing the myriad steps up the 1,448 m (4,750 ft) high Jade Dragon Peak. Two of the four viewing areas overlook the village and the others provide a vista over the crops on the floor beneath the peaks. It is now illegal to collect lotus leaves or roots within the park, but beyond its boundary, where cultivated lotus ponds jostle alongside the rice paddies, the tuberous roots are dug up in winter and eaten fried in thin slices. With such a bountiful resource, it is not surprising that other parts of the lotus are also used in local dishes. The leaves are made into an omelette, while the acorn-sized seeds go into a soup with pig bones or are mixed with rice to make a porridge.

Typically of karst landscapes the world over, the area is peppered with caves, but sadly, coloured naked strip lights on the walls provide the most uncreative lighting in any Chinese cave I have entered. The highlight of the day is a three-hour boat trip, but after seeing that the boats all carried up to eight people, I asked my guide, Sunny, if we could have a boat to ourselves. A quick call to her boss gained the necessary permission, provided I would do an interview with Yunnan Television, to which I readily agreed.

The cameraman positioned himself in one boat whilst I was in another with a young presenter and my two guides. The 'ten-minute' interview extended to an hour because the presenter had such a poor command of English that everything we both said had to

< The lotus
leaf emerges
sculpture-like,
with enrolled
margins, at the
water's surface.

< When it rains, drops of water appear like silver jewels – often arranged in lines along the veins – and are retained on the water-repellent surface of lotus leaves.

∨↵ After a foray in search of food or hawking back and forth within their territory, dragonflies return to a favourite resting place atop a lotus stem or leaf. The many species found at Puzhehei Hu include the male golden flange tail (*Sinictogomphus* sp.) below.

be translated by Sunny, who could have done a much better job at presenting. No matter, after I had deleted all the uncomposed shots I took so that the cameraman could record my clicking shutter, we had the boat to ourselves and our very willing boatman obligingly paddled across to every photogenic lotus I spied.

This was turning out to be a blissful afternoon until we rounded a corner and spotted a water fight between a couple of boats ahead. Plastic bowls and buckets, not to mention plastic and bamboo water guns, are sold in local shops and by traders beside the lake. By steering an avoiding course and with me standing up, looking very much the serious photographer with a long lens, we managed to avoid an attack. One boat was not so lucky and sank from the excessive water load. Fortunately, Immortal Lake averages only a couple of metres (6 ft 6 in) in depth and life jackets are compulsory.

I had high hopes of spotting an elegant pheasant-tailed jacana (*Hydrophasianus chirurgus*), but with so much commotion from the water fights, it was not surprising I had only a fleeting glimpse of a few wagtails, a mallard, a little grebe and a Chinese pond heron (*Ardeola bacchus*). The extensive lotus lakes are nonetheless awesome and must rank as one of the most spectacular aquatic scenes in Asia.

CHAPTER 4

CHINA'S NATIONAL TREASURE

When not sitting down to munch bamboo, giant pandas almost invariably amble over the ground with their pigeon-toed walk, though if the need arises they are quite capable of speeding up and breaking into a run. They are also adept at climbing trees, but some individuals relish this more than others. During several months in winter they have to trudge over snow-covered ground in search of bamboo. One moment a panda may be walking up a snowy slope and the next slipping and sliding ignominiously on its back with all four limbs up in the air, before righting itself and lumbering off into the forest.

< As a giant panda walks up a snowy slope at Wolong, it loses its footing and slithers down again. Researchers have seen tracks showing where pandas have tobogganned on their bellies down slopes covered with thick snow.

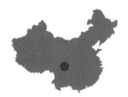

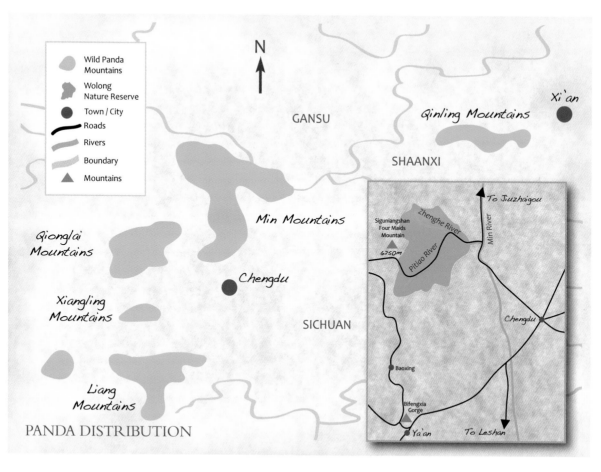

Legend:
- Wild Panda Mountains
- Wolong Nature Reserve
- Town / City
- Roads
- Rivers
- Boundary
- Mountains

N

GANSU

Qinling Mountains

Xi'an

SHAANXI

Min Mountains

Qionglai Mountains

Chengdu

Xiangling Mountains

SICHUAN

Liang Mountains

PANDA DISTRIBUTION

Siguniangshan Four Maids Mountain

6250m

Zhenghe River

Pitiao River

Min River

To Jiuzhaigou

Chengdu

Baoxing

Bifengxia Gorge

Ya'an

To Leshan

> When snow falls on bamboos, pandas shake the branches before starting to eat.

The giant panda is now confined to China, but fossil remains confirm that it used to live in northern Myanmar, Vietnam and a much wider area of southern and south-eastern China. Hunting and loss of habitat have pushed pandas further and further north to their present distribution: a small pocket of temperate forest across six mountain areas along the eastern rim of the Tibetan Plateau: the Minshan, Qinling, Qionglai, Liangshan, Daxiangling and Xiaoxiangling ranges. Typically pandas live within a vertical range of 1,500–3,000 m (4,900–9,800 ft), moving down in winter and up again into cooler mountain air in late spring, always seeking areas with a bountiful bamboo understorey.

No one outside China knew of the giant panda's existence until the French missionary and naturalist Père Armand David (1826–1900) spotted a panda skin on the floor of a Sichuan hunter's hut in 1869. Noting the bear-like characteristics, he assumed it was a carnivorous bear and named it *Ursus melanaoleuca*, but it was later renamed *Ailuropoda melanoleuca*.

62

< The giant panda is China's most iconic animal: the distinctive monochromatic colouring, clown-like face, black nose, eye patches and Mickey Mouse-like ears make it one of the most appealing and popular of the world's endangered species.

< Golden snub-nosed monkeys' eyes are surrounded by distinctive blue rings, but only the male, shown here, has long back hairs that fly skywards when he leaps from one tree to another. These monkeys live in troops in the same habitat as the giant panda.

Once Western museums heard about this intriguing new mammal, they were eager to sponsor hunters to gain a novel stuffed exhibit. David never saw a live panda and it was more than half a century after his discovery that the Western world set eyes on one. Just before Christmas 1936, a New York fashion designer named Ruth Harkness succeeded in bringing a young panda back to North America. So began the world's love affair with the animal known in China as *daxiongmao* (large bear cat). Zoos clamoured for them: a further 14 were captured by foreigners from 1936–46, at which time China prohibited the collection of any more. Later followed a period (1957–83) when no fewer than 24 pandas were donated to foreign countries as goodwill ambassadors.

During this time – in the 1960s – the first four panda reserves were established in China, the most famous being the Wolong NNR in Sichuan, set up in 1963. It contains deciduous and coniferous forests, river valleys, alpine slopes and high, glacier-covered mountain peaks, which harbour a profusion of plant types and countless birds and mammals, including colourful pheasants, the red or lesser panda, the golden snub-nosed monkey (*Rhinopithecus roxellana*), the musk deer and the takin, which all share the giant panda's terrain.

< A vertical rock provides a convenient back rest for
a panda sitting down to feed at Wolong in winter.

ᵛ Bamboo culm debris litters the ground beneath a feeding panda.
The underside of the foot shows the hairs and pads; the strong claws
are used to grip trees when climbing.

> Dusted with snow, a giant panda feasts on bamboo.

bamboo (*Fargesia robusta*), although their choice will vary
with the seasons. To save energy when feeding, they either
sit on the ground or lounge against a tree trunk or a gently
sloping bank with their hind feet outstretched. When
walking, a panda appears to bumble along, whereas when
it feeds it is able to manipulate a bamboo cane with great
dexterity by using an enlarged wrist bone – the so-called
pseudothumb – which functions as a sixth digit. After a
cane is severed near the base, the side shoots are nipped
off one by one and held in the mouth, with an enrolled
tongue keeping the base of the shoots together as a small
bunch. This is then transferred to a hand before being
eaten. After stripping the leaves, the panda's sharply
pointed canines slice efficiently through the woody stem.

Bamboos grow for several decades before they flower.
Then all the plants of one kind of bamboo within an area
flower at the same time and die, which results in a glut of
seed being produced; this overwhelms seed-eating animals,
ensuring that much of the seed survives. It is, however, bad
news for pandas living in isolated forest pockets, because
they are unable to move into new feeding areas when
the bamboo dies; they can literally starve to death. This
occurred during 1975–76, when a large area within the
Min Mountains suffered from simultaneous die-back of
three bamboo species; tragically, 138 panda bodies were
discovered. After the bamboo seeds germinate it can take
20 years before the plants are large enough to support
pandas. It is not known why bamboo die-back occurs,
although the seedlings may need the light gained after the
collapse of the mature bamboo canopy in order to grow.

Fossil evidence indicates that pandas were originally
carnivorous, but gradually, as they began to eat more
bamboo and less meat, they led a less active life, making
them less capable of hunting down prey. Present-day
pandas, however, still appreciate the chance to eat carrion.
George Schaller found golden snub-nosed monkey hair
in one panda dropping, and the hair, bones and hooves
of musk deer in another. Pandas have retained a short,
carnivorous gut which (unlike that of cattle, which
harbours microscopic organisms) is unable to break down
the cell walls of plants, with the result that a panda digests
only 12–23 per cent of the bamboo
it eats. This means that, unlike bears,
pandas cannot lay down food
reserves and are unable to hibernate
in winter. So, day in, day out
throughout the year – regardless
of the weather – a panda spends up
to 14 hours in 24 consuming on
average 19 kg (42 lb) of bamboo.

Several different kinds of
bamboo grow in the Wolong NNR;
pandas prefer arrow bamboo
(*Bashania fangiana*) and umbrella

In 1983, when arrow bamboo
flowered throughout Wolong, some
85 per cent died and a few pandas
starved, but a research team noticed
that most of them became less
selective and moved down the
mountain to feed on umbrella
bamboo. So, provided a choice of
bamboo is available, pandas should
be able to survive a die-back crisis,
unless all the main food species
happen to flower at the same time,
as they did in the Min Mountains.

Extensive forest destruction by logging and, at lower elevations, clearance for agriculture led to 50 per cent of the panda's habitat being lost in Sichuan province alone between 1974 and 1989. Also in Sichuan, Chinese officials recovered the pelts of 146 pandas in 1988. Even though the penalty for poaching a panda is a 20-year prison sentence, the reward for a pelt is so great that some people are prepared to risk it. Pandas may also accidentally be injured or killed in traps and snares set for other animals, including musk deer and black bears.

In 1998, the Chinese government declared a ban on logging, which has relieved one of the biggest threats to giant pandas, as well as making the restoration of degraded forest habitat a real possibility. Obtaining an accurate estimate of the total wild panda population is difficult in mountainous country and for years it was thought to be around 1,000. However, by the time the third National Panda Survey was completed in 2004, electronic tracking devices and GPS enabled a team of over 170 scientists, field workers and conservationists traversing remote and rugged mountains to conclude that the wild population totalled 1,600 pandas. This sounds encouraging, but the elevated figure may be due to more accurate methods of counting rather than a marked increase in the population.

^ Growing beside a waterfall, a bamboo plant became encased in ice as splashing water froze over it. Many rock faces in Wolong are decorated with dagger-like icicles in winter.

^ Wolong is now a UNESCO Man and Biosphere protected area; its forests are among the most biologically rich temperate areas on Earth. With increasing altitude, the deciduous forest gives way to conifers which are covered with a mantle of snow for much of the winter.

My first trip to Wolong was in 1984; we stayed in a local school, but saw no pandas. In those days it was a tortuous journey along a bone-crunching road following the Pitiao River. Since then, I have visited Wolong many times, appreciating improvements both to the road and in the accommodation. By 1995, the huge, newly opened Panda Hotel looked promising, with *en suite* bathrooms, but a distinct smell of mould pervaded everywhere from leaking pipes. Many showers and toilets either failed to work or else gushed water continually. Two years later, I made my first winter trip, to photograph pandas in the snow at the China Conservation and Research Center for the Giant Panda (CCRCGP). This time my base was a newish hotel – already with defective plumbing and electrics – where I was the sole guest. The cook had departed for the Chinese New Year, the food was sparse and the temperature in my room never rose above 5°C in ten days! But with spectacular scenery I was happy to remain outside from dawn to dusk.

Spring, being more congenial, is a glorious season to be in Wolong. Rhododendrons flower in the forest and the deciduous trees leaf out

∧ A close view of a panda's face shows the distinctive black patches that surround each eye, with a dusting of snow on the chin. Fortunately none of the panda's body parts are sought after for TCM.

∟ Many kinds of rhododendron flower in spring, bringing splashes of colour to the Wolong forests.

in a wide range of colours before they turn a uniform dull green. But the whole area was shattered on 12 May 2008 when the worst earthquake to hit China for over three decades had its epicentre 10 km (6 miles) from Wolong. People on a British tour at the Panda Center at the time later related how one minute the pandas were happily feeding and the next they suddenly stopped and became agitated. Shortly afterwards rocks came hurtling down the mountainside. Of the 32 panda enclosures, 14 were buried or totally destroyed and the other 18 severely damaged, but amazingly only one animal was crushed to death. Another was injured and two escaped, but one of those returned. Staff relate how many pandas raced up into tree tops and refused to come down – a sign of stress. The quake was possibly a reason why fewer pandas were born at Wolong in 2008 – 13, compared with 17 in 2007.

67

Gradually, the Wolong pandas were relocated. A total of 38 were eventually transferred to Bifengxia CCRCGP, which lies south of Wolong near Ya'an, at a lower and warmer altitude. It opened in December 2003 with the aim of safeguarding against the risk of disease spreading through the captive pandas at Wolong. Others went to the Chengdu Research Base of Giant Panda Breeding (CRBGPB), founded in 1987, and to zoos in various Chinese cities. Six 18-month-old pandas were relocated to a safer place within Wolong, to reassure local people that others will return to their valley after a new panda centre is built and that the bamboo which local farmers have grown recently as a year-round cash crop for panda fodder will once again become profitable.

The precipitous terrain makes it difficult to assess how many wild pandas suffered as a result of the earthquake, but since it is known to have killed nearly 69,000 people, with a further 18,000 missing, it is probable that some pandas

were injured, if not killed, by flying rocks, while others may have had difficulty gaining access to essential bamboo in places where landslides blocked familiar paths.

In the early days, attempts at breeding pandas in captivity had a low success rate and it was erroneously assumed that wild pandas were also poor breeders. When captive animals failed to mate, researchers resorted to showing them blue movies of pandas mating to get them in the mood; nowadays artificial insemination is used if a natural mating fails. Recently, long-term studies of wild pandas have shown that their reproductive rates are comparable to those of some thriving American black bear populations. A newborn panda weighs around 100 g (3.5 oz) and is pink and rat-like with an obvious tail; black fur does not begin to appear until three weeks. There are now almost 300 captive-bred pandas – mostly in China, with a few in zoos around the world. These zoos pay the Chinese government one million US dollars a year under the rent-

<< By five months, a baby giant panda looks like a small replica of an adult but it has a lot to learn – such as how to climb over obstacles and up trees and, not least, how to process bamboo.

< Giant panda cubs play-fighting in the snow at Wolong.

ᵛ At Bifengxia CCRCGP, near Ya'an, a panda rests on the base of a branch after climbing a tree in winter.

a-panda scheme, whereby a pair of pandas is loaned for ten years, but all offspring belong to China and are eventually returned there.

Experts first met in 1991 to consider the possibilities of reintroducing pandas into the wild, but it was not until 2006 that a five-year-old male fitted with a radio collar was released at Wolong. He survived for less than a year and the postmortem indicated that he had fallen from a rock – maybe after a fight with another male panda. The earthquake has set back the programme for teaching pandas the skills necessary for survival in the wild, but work has now begun on the new CCRCGP at Huangcaoping. Located in a scenic valley within the Wolong NNR, about 10 km (6 miles) from the original centre, it will include extensive natural enclosures for giant pandas, a veterinary hospital, a laboratory, a panda nursery, a cub play yard, a bamboo plantation and a site for introducing pandas into the wild.

69

< As a giant panda walks along a forest path in Wolong the huge head, which contains outsized strong jaw muscles necessary for chewing tough bamboo, is carried low. Recent DNA research has proved that Père David's assumption that pandas were bears is correct.

> Resting against a tree trunk a panda's flexible body enables it to scratch its head using a hind foot.

With the Wolong centre closed, I was curious to see the Bifengxia CCRCGP set-up and spent several days there with a small group from the USA early in 2010. This scenic area consists of two main attractions – the panda centre and a safari-park-type zoo where you are transported on a bus through areas with big game. Access to the entrance of the panda area is also via a bus, from where you either walk along tarmac paths or pay to ride in an electric cart. Pandas emerge from their houses to feed in large natural forest enclosures, where some climb trees. In winter we had difficulty getting a good view of the pandas whenever a Chinese group turned up, so in the peak season the prime viewing points are likely to be very crowded, unless you have an early start on a weekday. Our accommodation, euphemistically referred to as 'villas', did have *en suite* facilities, but hot water never emerged during the three days we were there and the cold water permanently resembled a muddy stream. On the plus side, however, there were electric blankets on the beds. Until the new centre is built at Wolong, Bifengxia CCRCGP and the Chengdu base will be the best places to see several pandas in large enclosures.

Although there are now more than 60 panda reserves, some are small, which may cause inbreeding. So, to enhance the gene flow, as well as to counteract the problem of starvation from bamboo die-back, bamboo corridors are being planted. Pandas will be able to travel along these from one reserve to another, continuing to feed on their way to an alternative food source and perhaps finding a mate.

Since the World Wide Fund for Nature (WWF) was invited by the Chinese government to collaborate with panda conservation in 1979, it has been involved in many panda-based and other projects in China. In March 2002 the Qinling Panda Focal Project was launched to help the small Qinling panda population (200–300 animals), which has little connection to other populations. The project involves habitat protection and the creation of five ecological corridors, as well as co-operation between biodiversity conservation and tourism development in one area and sustainable community development for all the Qinling giant panda range. WWF has supported farmers in various ways here: traditional bee hives have been replaced with new ones that do not require new logs every year and five households have been selected to develop home-stays for eco-tourists, which avoids land being cleared for building a hotel.

Many people are now beavering away towards a common goal, namely the long-term survival of giant pandas in the wild. As a result of enhanced and enlarged reserves, bamboo corridors, tougher anti-poaching control and the re-introduction of captive pandas, it is to be hoped that China's national treasure will continue to roam the mountain ranges for many generations to come.

CHAPTER 5

HOT SPRINGS AND RAINFORESTS

When my guide, Mr Ling, replaced the plastic beach shoes he had worn on the previous afternoon's forest walk with laced canvas boots, I knew our next outing was not going to be a stroll in the park. This would be real trekking on Gaoligongshan, an elongated mountain range lying in south-west China, with its west flank bordering Myanmar. After planning the trip for a couple of years, I was eager to explore this exceptionally rich area, where few Westerners – apart from plant hunters and botanists – have set foot.

< Sunrise from Gaoligongshan – part of the Three Parallel Rivers WHS – breaking through a gap in the clouds near Baihualing ranger station.

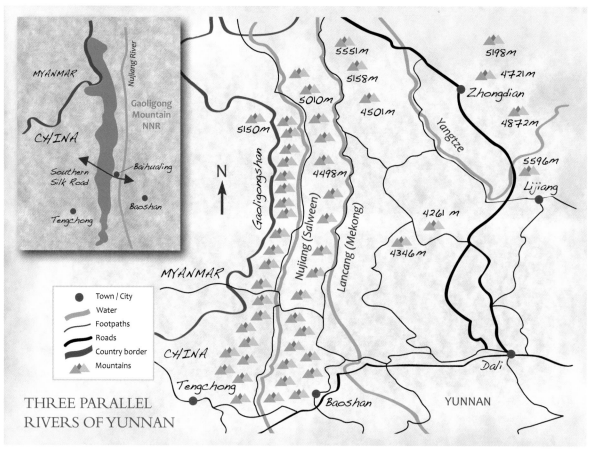

THREE PARALLEL
RIVERS OF YUNNAN

An area of high mountains with steep valleys was
formed in the north-eastern part of Yunnan
province when the Indian subcontinental plate collided
with the Eurasian plate some 40 million years ago. Four
mountain ranges separate three mighty rivers which start
life on the Qinghai-Tibet Plateau and run parallel for
170 km (106 miles). The Jinsha River ultimately becomes
the Yangtze; the Lancang becomes the Mekong of South-
East Asia, while the Nujiang flows into the Salween in
Myanmar and Thailand. It is the topography of this
region – known as the Three Parallel Rivers – that has
produced a biodiversity 'hotspot' and World Heritage
Site. The figures are impressive: more than 20 per
cent of the flowering plants and over 24 per
cent of the animal species found in the whole
of China occur in this region, a mere 4 per
cent of the country's land mass.

When mountain ranges run in a
west-east direction, they act as natural
barriers to the north-south

movement of species, especially after periods of glaciation.
The Three Parallel Rivers valleys run north-south, which
allowed plant and animal species to move south during
the ice ages, when Gaoligongshan's year-round mild
climate provided a refuge for many plants and some
primates. After the ice retreated, plants and animals alike
were able to disperse throughout the valleys, which also
act as funnels, drawing up warm moist air from the south.

Straddling 24° 56' to 26° 09' N latitude and lying close
to the frigid Tibetan Plateau, Gaoligongshan might
be expected to have a temperate forest covering. But
with the Nujiang running along the eastern flank,
it is fed by humid air from tropical South-East Asia,
so that the lower slopes are covered in evergreen
broad-leaved rainforest, complete with leeches.
As one moves up the mountain, temperate species begin
to appear, with alpine plants above. Humid conditions at
higher levels encourage rich mossy growths on tree trunks
and branches, with an array of flowering epiphytes that
provide nectar for hummingbirds.

^ A narrow path at higher levels on Gaoligongshan passes through trees with copious epiphytes on their trunks and branches.

> An attractive flower head growing as a flat-topped umbel was not uncommon beside the path around the mid-altitude.

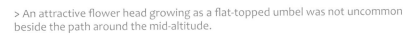

< The red panda occurs in forests with bamboo thickets between 2,000 and 3,700 m (6,500–12,000 ft) on Gaoligongshan, which was designated a National Nature Reserve in 1986. This panda feeds mainly on bamboo, but it also raids birds' nests for eggs and nestlings. The long bushy tail provides a warm wrap at higher altitudes.

> Several kinds of flower are used in stir-fry dishes in Yunnan, such as these bird flowers (*Polygala arillata*) on sale in a Tengchong market.

ᵛ One of the few rhododendrons in bloom in late April.

The American plant hunter Dr Joseph Rock (1884–1962), travelling with an army of porters and pack ponies, was the first Westerner to discover the rich flora on Gaoligongshan. Since then, the plant list has continued to grow with each successive botanical expedition. The wildlife is no less diverse, with a large proportion of China's pheasants, the red or lesser panda and the white-browed or hoolock gibbon (*Hoolock leuconedys*) all making their home here.

This gibbon has recently been placed in its own genus, *Hoolock*. Like the white-cheeked gibbon (see Chapter 8), males are blackish, but with a white strip above the eyes instead of down the cheeks; adult females range from buff to various shades of tan with a black face. The humidity ensures that fruit remains on the trees year round, providing food for the gibbons and other monkeys as well as squirrels, including the black giant or Malayan giant squirrel (*Ratufa bicolor*), which can reach almost 1 m (3 ft) long.

Chinese natural history books, with even minimal English text, are hard to come by in China, so I always make a beeline for bookshops in the larger cities. In Kunming I found a book on this special mountain, where photographs of huge tree-like rhododendrons, bearing a canopy of red blooms above trunks festooned with epiphytic mosses, caught my eye – one of those 'must-see' botanical spectacles. Several botanists told me that April was the prime flowering time.

The remoteness of the area has made it difficult for outsiders to visit and only recently has the reserve been opened up to ecotourism. Now it is possible to trek across the mountain from Baoshan to Tengchong (a border town with Myanmar, south-west of Dali) following the ancient southern Silk Road.

During the second Sino-Japanese War (1937–45), Tengchong was a main battlefield. The section of the Burma Road from Kunming to the Burmese border was built in harsh mountainous country by 200,000 Chinese labourers, without any machinery, in just nine months from 1937 to 1938 and became an important supply line when Burma was still a British colony. But when the Japanese seized several parts of Burma in 1942, this effectively cut Allied access to the road. An airbridge was developed over the Himalayas and the Gaoligongshan range to maintain supplies between Bengal and Yunnan; it became known as the Hump Airlift because the planes often had to fly between two peaks that resembled camel humps.

Early in 2009, a new commercial airport opened at Tengchong; it was named Hump Airport and the approach road the Flying Tigers Road in memory of the American pilots who flew the route. I decided to spend a few days in Tengchong – once a highly active geothermal region – before visiting Gaoligongshan. The 97 dormant volcanic cones (now clothed in vegetation) and exposed hexagonal basalt columns, formed from condensed magma, are testimony to past activity. Hot springs, still active today, are a tourist attraction as well as being valued for their healing properties.

Within the Hot Springs Sea area, I was disappointed to find no spectacular geysers erupting skywards, just bubbling springs and boiling pools. The main attraction is Dagunguo, a large hot spring that reaches 97°C (206°F) or more. Where water ran down a multi-coloured sinter apron – a crust formed from silicon and sulphur deposits – a butterfly was sipping water and minerals at the base. This reminded me of a chance meeting I had with an aged amateur entomologist early one morning on a Peruvian riverbank. Clutching an empty sardine tin partially filled with liquid, he looked somewhat sheepish as he explained that urine was a marvellous attractant for butterflies!

Later, flicking through a book on Tengchong, I saw a wetland with sheets of purple-flowered irises. Emma, my English-speaking guide, agreed we could go to Beihai wetland; as luck would have it, it was the peak time for

these flowers. This unscheduled visit was a complete delight as I walked along boardwalks with a skylark singing overhead, before being rowed through open water channels where water buffalo bathed in the shallows, with others in the distance grazing on the floating marshy carpet – no doubt with their mouths full of iris flowers.

From Tengchong, it takes only a few hours to drive to Gaoligong. When we reached the Nujiang Basin, roadside stalls stocked with mangoes and bananas were proof that we had entered a warmer climate zone. As we ascended the lower slopes of Gaoligongshan, the bananas gave way to coffee plantations. These petered out as we reached the gates of Baihualing ranger station (my home for six nights) on the east of the Gaoligong range. Mr Ling, the manager of the station, was to be my guide, but apparently spoke no English; however Emma had kindly translated into Chinese questions I had written in my

< Steam rises from the water of Dagunguo, the Big Boiling Pot, within the Hot Springs Sea area at Tengchong National Geopark.

^ At Beihai wetland near Tengchong, a succession of flowers erupts through a floating marshy carpet on a barrier lake formed from molten lava disgorged by volcanic eruptions. After pale pink spikes of bogbean fade, swathes of deep-purple irises transform this wetland in the latter part of April.

> Flowers on the *Melastoma polyanthum* shrub survive steam wafting around them from a thermal spring in the Hot Springs Sea area.

↲ Iris flowering at Beihai wetland in April.

notebook about mealtimes and the plants that I sought.

Before she departed, I needed confirmation that the giant rhododendrons would be in flower. It was a great blow to discover I was two months too late, although in some ways this felt better than missing them by a couple of weeks. It transpired that Mr Ling did have some basic English, which revolved around drinking and eating. Shortly after I arrived, he came to my room announcing *a cup of tea*; not long afterwards, *lunch* was declared with great relish and later *supper*.

^ The Southern Silk Road runs outside the core area of Gaoligongshan NNR and passes near Baihualing ranger station.

< Phayre's leaf monkey (*Trachypithecus phayrei*) lives in trees and feeds on leaves, flowers and fruits early and late in the day. It is found in groups of 10 to 60 at around 2,000–2,800 m (6,500–9,200 ft) on Gaoligongshan.

> One of many waterfalls that cascade over rocks in Gaoligongshan, where the water flow becomes thunderous during the monsoon season.

My room, one of many used by visiting scientists, was built around a central courtyard and fairly basic, with a large desk plus electric sockets so I could recharge camera batteries, a downloader, mobile phone and laptop. That night I awoke in a semi-stupor, feeling an insect crawling over my arm, and was relieved to find it was only a cockroach, not a bedbug. On virtually every trip to China, I am bitten by bedbugs at least once – including in one of the most famous hotels in Shanghai. Cockroaches are less of a nuisance: they scavenge but do not suck blood.

Without a local map, I was completely in the dark as to where we were going each day, but I was heartened to note that after an initial trek up the same newly widened road we set off in a different direction every time.

Walking the ancient tea and horse road was hard work. In essence no more than a track, parts of it still boasted stone slabs worn smooth by the repeated tramping of both human and horses' feet; and these were treacherous, whether covered with dry leaves or after rain. Sometimes

the track levelled out and was clothed with a thick layer of leaves that made it not unlike an amble through an English beech wood in the autumn – except that the leaves of many of the evergreen trees (which are shed throughout the year) were much thicker and larger. In other parts, stone risers came almost up to my knees and it was almost impossible to surmount them until Mr Ling cut me a walking pole.

Each valley had a distinct collection of plants – some unique to a single valley. My first whole day in the field was a 'waterfall day', when small black flies swarmed around our heads and cameras, entering every orifice – worst of all, our eyes. I soon learnt to walk around with my eyes reduced to narrow slits, but then I could not see the plants clearly and I certainly could not focus the camera. Before exposing each frame, I had to wave my hand frantically in front of the lens to shoo the flies away. That evening, a fruitful ferret through my bag unearthed an Australian fly net.

At this time of year, just before the start of the monsoon rains, the Gaoligong falls had yet to become raging torrents, so that mossy carpets were visible behind them. Another advantage of coming now was that I failed to pick up a single leech: they don't begin actively searching for hosts to latch onto until the wet season.

< At higher levels the paths were littered with deep-pink rhododendron flowers fallen from tall, spindly trees. The open branches are visited by outsized bees that busily buzz their way from one flower to the next.

In the heart of the forest it was a surprise to discover a spring pool with the temperature of a pleasantly hot bath. Mr Ling had come prepared and stripped off to his bathers. Without my costume, I had to make do with a feeble paddle, but I was more intrigued to record a variety of butterflies coming to drink at thermal seeps.

Spotting wildlife in a dense rainforest is never easy. Quite apart from the different layers, many branches and creepers produce vertical leafy curtains. Wildlife photography therefore involves either a great investment in time – working along trails that some animals pass regularly – or a huge amount of luck. On my second full day in the forest, I was very fortunate to see two black giant squirrels racing along branches high up in separate trees. Throughout the day, the melody of bird and insect calls varied from one location to another.

Like all my Chinese guides, Mr Ling made and received calls on his mobile throughout the day, but when he later began to play music on it, I put my hands over my ears and he got the message. He was always willing to please and concerned for my safety. He loved the sound of my continuous motor drive and as soon as I took the camera off the tripod he scooped it up and was firing off shots left, right and centre. Fortunately, using digital cameras meant I could delete his pictures later.

Climbing up the mountain, I had spotted discarded plastic bags and bottles, so on the way down I began to collect rubbish. Mr Ling indicated with a wave of his hand that this was unnecessary. The following morning he gesticulated that his wife would accompany me up the mountain, when we would aim for the summit. We spent a long time walking up the new road and, as the heat increased, I was wishing

< A China nawab butterfly (*Polyura narcaeus*) drinks at a thermal seep in the heart of Gaoligongshan forest.

> The five-portioned fruits of a *Sterculia* tree look for all the world like starfish dangling from the sky.

< Copious fruits on fig trees provide food for monkeys and squirrels.

ᵛ Large combs made by wild honeybees are protected from the elements beneath the shelter of a rocky overhang.

I had one of those pith helmets with a built-in solar-powered fan, which I had always scorned when I had seen them worn on safari in East Africa. Now I realised that one would have helped cool me down and might even have diverted the flies from my face.

The contrast between the end of the new road and the beginning of a narrow jeep track was staggering. Gone were the bare banks. Instead, trees arched over on both sides to shade the track and the bankside was festooned with outsized fern fronds reaching a couple of metres (6–7 ft) in length, interspersed with cascading white-flowered hydrangeas. The blobby hydrangea heads with massed pink or blue flowers that appear in some English garden centres have never appealed to me, but in our Surrey garden we grow a stunning Chinese hydrangea with an outer ring of sterile white bracts surrounding a mass of tiny purple flowers that attract a host of insect pollinators.

^ Tightly coiled fern crosiers emerge from a bank beside the track, eventually opening out into large fronds.

ˇ A panoramic view of large bamboo clumps gracefully arching over at over 2,000 m (6,500 ft).

Although Mrs Ling knew even less English than her husband, it did not take her long to cotton on to how I worked and she was pointing out unusual plants all the way along the route. She spotted the first tree fern in a valley where they clearly thrived, and several interesting fruiting trees, as well as a snake, which I guess she had heard rustling dry leaves.

Rounding a bend we came upon a stand of plants that I had seen growing at Kew and at Inverewe garden in Scotland, but had waited years to find in the wild. Here at last was a variety of the famed giant Himalayan lily (*Cardiocrinum giganteum*), discovered in 1821 by the plant hunter Nathaniel Wallich in the eastern Himalayas. Some of the spikes reached up to 2 m (6 ft 6 in) tall, so it would have been hard to miss them. Most were still in bud, but further up the path we found two stands growing beneath conifers, where I could scramble down to look inside a waxy flower for the distinctive deep purple-red markings and to breathe in the fragrant smell.

After we had trekked for almost six hours (with frequent photo stops), it began to rain. Not knowing how far the summit was, I thought it prudent to turn

> A caterpillar munches a fern frond on Gaoligongshan. Its urticating hairs can cause a skin rash.

⌐ Giant Himalayan lilies (*Cardiocrinum giganteum* var. *yunnanense*) begin to flower on Gaoligongshan in early May.

back, because water on any vital electronic connection can be a problem. Once again, I could not resist picking up litter during our descent. This time Mrs Ling was eager to vie with me as to who could collect the more.

Each day Mr Ling had promised 'bus tomorrow', so I was heartened when a small pick-up appeared before 7 a.m. on my last day to speed us up the barren new road. We set off in high spirits, only to come to a grinding halt around the third bend, faced with piles of cobbles dumped in our path. As we plodded up the road, I could ignore all the plants I had already seen and we were on a new part of the track within three hours. By then, bamboos were beginning to appear between the tall trees and drifts of iris leaves bordered the paths.

> A yellow-flowering epiphytic orchid blown off a tree high up in the canopy.

ⱽ Striking deep-purple *Mucuna* flowers grow directly from the woody liana trunks.

Scattered across one stretch of the path were the dramatic purple-black waxy flowers of a liana known as *Mucuna*. Gazing upwards I could see bunches of some 20 outsized, pea-like blooms growing directly from thick trunks. I pondered why the flowers were such a dark colour. Did they have a foetid smell that attracted pollinators or did the flowers reflect ultraviolet light that we could not see? Following the long aerial roots hanging down from the woody lianas, I noticed that they snaked their way over the ground – a fraction too late to prevent one wrapping itself around my bare ankles beneath my trousers. That night I discovered huge red welts had appeared around my ankles, almost hot enough to fry an egg. Belatedly, I remembered that the seed pods of the velvet bean (*Mucuna pruriens*) are covered in loose orange hairs that cause itchy blisters if they come in contact with skin.

At higher levels, clouds frequently envelop the peaks, increasing the humidity and making everything appear lusher than it does lower down. Here, epiphytic mosses coat tree trunks along their entire length. Upper branches support an array of flowering plants, including orchids. Prior to the monsoon season (May to September), gales rage through the forest, ripping rotten branches festooned with orchids and sending them crashing to the ground. I had envisaged getting shots of the orchids *in situ*, but the trees were so tall that a 400mm lens was hopelessly inadequate. Freshly grounded plants provided the closest view possible.

By the time we walked through the gates of Baihualing ranger station we had been trekking for 11 hours in unquestionably the most intriguing forest I had ever experienced in China. What is more, I had even converted Mr Ling to picking up rubbish! Gaoligongshan is an important gene bank of many rare species, so it is vital that care is taken to ensure pressure from tourism does not threaten this unique area. I shall return to see the glorious red-flowering rhododendron trees.

^ One of the four species of macaque found on Gaoligongshan is the pig-tailed macaque (*Macaca nemestrina*), which eats fruits, leaves, insects and small birds. The distinct crest on the top of this one's head identifies it as a male.

CHAPTER 6

KARST, CAVES, CORMORANTS AND CARP

The entrance to the cave is narrow, and winding paths take you past several unmemorable formations lit by coloured lights until you eventually reach a cavern with a low ceiling above and a shallow lake below. It is not the conventional elongated stalactites and stalagmites that are the attraction here; instead, rare circular stalagmite formations seem to float on the water. Over one hundred circular basins reminiscent of lotus leaves appear just above the waterline as the jewels in the crown.

< The Lotus Basin Cave in Bai Shan Di Village near Xingping is very special – it contains 108 limestone basins which resemble lotus leaves in water.

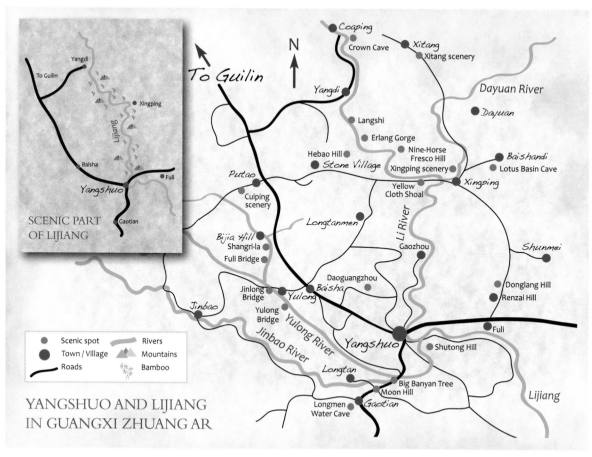

SCENIC PART
OF LIJIANG

Legend:
- Scenic spot
- Town / Village
- Roads
- Rivers
- Mountains
- Bamboo

YANGSHUO AND LIJIANG
IN GUANGXI ZHUANG AR

Above the ground, karst landscapes vary from towers or peaks to flattened limestone pavement – all created by the action of water on limestone. When rain falls it absorbs some carbon dioxide from the air to form a weak acid, which permeates and widens cracks in the limestone. Over eons of time, copious run-off water, together with underground rivers, hollows out the subterranean part of karst formations.

The term karst derives from the Slovenian *kras*, meaning a bleak, waterless place. It was first used to describe a landscape formed by the erosion of carbonate rocks such as limestone and dolomite in the Dinaric Alps in the former Yugoslavia. Today it is applied to similar features all over the world.

South China is one of the world's major karst landscapes, with the Guilin and Yangshuo area in Guangxi Zhuang AR being one of the most extensive. For centuries it has lured many artists and, more recently, photographers. In 1982 it became the Guilin and Lijiang River National Park.

Several hundred million years ago, this area was a gulf where limestone deposits built up from the remains of marine plants and animals that gradually accumulated beneath the sea. When the land was later uplifted, the limestone bedrock became eroded by rain, wind and flowing water, leaving the peaks and pinnacles that now dominate the charismatic landscape above a hidden world of dramatic caverns.

Southern or south-west China has countless cave systems with an array of different formations that may have taken anything from a few hundred to a million years to form. Inside the caves, where water rich in dissolved calcium drips from the ceilings, the calcium becomes redeposited, forming stalactites that hang down from the ceilings and stalagmites that grow up from the floor. If they eventually join up, they become columns. Stalactites and stalagmites are so variable in their shape and colour that no two are identical. Their growth rates are so slow that, if they are damaged, they cannot possibly regrow within a human life span.

^ Subterranean waterfalls erode rock in a similar way
to waterfalls above ground; here is a rare underground
twin waterfall inside Jiuxiang Cave in Yunnan.

> The iconic karst scenery that backs the Lijiang (Li River)
in the Yangshuo area, with clumps of phoenix-tail bamboo
used to make the rafts that ply the river, is one of the
most photographed scenic landscapes in China.

^ A blind subterranean fish, *Sinocyclocheilus*, from Jiuxiang Cave has a distinct head bump and barbels but no eyes.

Over evolutionary time, a specialised cave fauna has evolved, able to live and breed in perpetual darkness where the ability to feel is the prime sense. Cave crickets sport outsized antennae and blind fish living in underground pools have well developed barbels that enable them to feel their way along the bottom. Little work has been done on China's cave fauna but, whenever animals have been collected, up to 90 per cent has been found to be new to science.

Caves can be opened up to tourists only after paths and steps have been laid and lighting installed. This inevitably leads to some damage, as well as to changes to the cave environment. Tourists themselves exacerbate the gradual destruction by affecting the humidity and the airflow, by creating dust and by touching the accessible formations.

Permanent features on the tourist circuit between Guilin and Yangshuo are Reed Flute Cave and the Music Cave, both of which have an array of fine stalactite and stalagmite formations. Close to the famous Moon Hill is the newly opened Longmen Water Cave at Gaotian: the longest cave in this area, it runs beneath no fewer than three karst towers.

To enter this sparsely lit cave with its low ceiling, a torch and a helmet are obligatory. Entry is by boat along a shallow river. As you leave the boat you have to stoop repeatedly along a wet and sometimes muddy pathway which climbs up to the beginning of the formations. Pictures can be taken using flash; but hand-holding a head torch, powered with LED bulbs, enabled me to paint light in a more creative way. Farther on, it is possible to swim in the refreshing water of the cave, to take a shower under a waterfall and bathe in liquid mud, but with so much photographic gear we opted out of the longer tour. During World War II local people used this cave as a hideout from the invading Japanese army and today it is still home to bats.

But the Lotus Basin Cave near Xingping is my favourite. When eight circular limestone basins were found within a cave in the former Yugoslavia half a century ago, they were considered a marvel of nature and thought to be unique. Years later no fewer than 108 such basins were discovered in the Lotus Basin Cave. Not until a Chinese geologist visited in 1984 was the importance of this cavern realised. He called the

<< A view of the Lotus Basin Cave with stalactites and stalagmites reflected in the shallow lake with two lotus basins.

< Longmen Water Cave at Gaotian is such an extensive system that it takes three hours to explore the cave formations, underground streams and waterfalls fully. Here stalactites have fused with stalagmites to form a column.

ᵛ The same view of the Lotus Basin Cave taken two years after the picture at the start of this chapter. Most of the green lights have burnt out, producing a more naturalistic view of the formations with the lower water revealing more of the basins.

formations lotus basins because they occur in water and resemble lotus leaves in an outdoor pond. Known elsewhere as lily pads, they form around existing stalagmites as shelves at or below the water surface. As new deposits are added at the air/water/rock interface the basins grow upwards as well as increasing their diameter. The unusual formations develop within an enclosed pool behind a rimstone dam of carbonate-rich deposits that build up at the edge of the pool as carbon dioxide escapes into the air.

Because the Lotus Basin Cave is off the tourist map, it is rarely visited, but the caretaker unlocked it and switched the lights on for us to explore and photograph on our own. On my first visit during the winter, the warm humid atmosphere underground had caused my glasses, camera lenses and viewfinder to steam up, so all had to be wiped before each shot, but this time there were no problems because the temperature outside and inside the cave were very similar.

There are several viewpoints known to photographers for the best scenics within the Yangshuo area. I was fortunate to get Pan Shijun to organise my trip and be my guide, as he lives in Yangshuo, is a keen photographer and has run many photo tours in the area. We had planned to visit different overviews at first and last light each day, but were thwarted by the haze produced by farmers burning the rice straw. Towards the end of my stay we decided to try Hebao Hill and rose at 4.30 a.m., in time to drive there and climb the hill just as dawn was breaking. All we could see were pathetic misty smudges of peaks; the winding river below was barely discernible. It was particularly galling when the local guide, whom we had picked up to unlock the gate blocking the ill-hewn rock path, showed me some stunning shots he had taken earlier in the year on his point-and-shoot camera – but then he must have been up dozens of times.

Other famous and much-visited Chinese karst landscapes include the World Heritage Sites of Jiuzhaigou and Huanglong (Yellow Dragon) in Sichuan and Shilin in Yunnan. Jiuzhaigou and Huanglong look nothing like the pinnacles around Guilin. Instead they are high-altitude valleys where travertine deposits result in cascading waterfalls and beautiful terraces. These deposits are formed as a result of eroded limestone producing carbonate-rich waters that flow down the valley,

^ Water tumbles down moss-covered calcareous deposits on the Arrow Bamboo waterfall in Jiuzhaigou.

> Extensive weathering of limestone peaks in the Stone Forest (Shilin) Geopark have resulted in sharp-edged karst.

>> Part of the upper travertine terrace within the karst landscape at Huanglong. The intense colours of the pools are caused by the high calcium bicarbonate content in the water.

94

redepositing the carbonates as a series of dams to create the terraces. Huanglong has the largest open travertine landscape in the world with 3,300 terraced pools ranging in colour from blue through green and yellow to a delicate milky white.

Access up Jiuzhaigou is via an efficient system of eco-friendly buses capable of bringing in 1.5 million people a year. However, since a major bridge was lost in the 2008 Sichuan earthquake, the road journey has become tedious and tortuous. At Huanglong, the easiest way to reach the stunning multi-coloured pools, contained within the top

travertine terrace, is to take the cable car and walk up the gentle incline on the boardwalk through the forest before making a final ascent to almost 3,600 m (11,800 ft). The speediest way down is to use the most direct boardwalks, which pass yet more travertine terraces.

Shilin Geopark, part of the multiple-location South China Karst WHS, is a karst landform laid down beneath the sea 270 million years ago. Movement of the crust and the gradual retreat of water caused the seabed to rise up, exposing sword-shaped peaks and stone clusters – hence the alternative name of Stone Forest.

Weaving around the base of the karst pinnacles in the Yangshuo area are the Li and Yangshuo Rivers, both famous locations for cormorant fishing. This traditional skill has been practised in China for more than one thousand years. Cormorants are also used by Japanese fishermen, who capture wild birds and train them. The Chinese birds, on the other hand, are fully domesticated, being bred, reared (by domestic hens) and trained by the fishermen. The Li River men work from a bamboo raft on which the birds and a basket are transported. Many fish at night using a light to attract the fish, but some use a net to corral the fish so that the cormorants can dive in and collect them by day.

I photographed Mr Chong Gui Huang at work: via Pan, I learnt that he had been taught by his grandfather and began fishing on the Li when he was seventeen. A cormorant can fish for 15 years; thereafter its eyesight deteriorates so it cannot see the prey easily. There are two periods in the year when the birds have a rest: in January, when the water is a bit cold, and during the summer rains, when the rivers flood.

<< A Li River fisherman, wearing a rain cape made from palm-leaf bases, on his bamboo raft with cormorants at dawn. The karst scenery forms a dramatic backdrop.

⌐ A fisherman constricts the cormorant's neck with rice straw so it cannot swallow large fish.

^ A trained cormorant emerges with a partially swallowed fish.

˅ A cormorant, its neck tied to prevent it swallowing fish, stands on a raft with outstretched wings to dry them off because their feathers are not waterproofed.

Working from his bamboo raft, Mr Huang went through a ritual he has followed for almost half a century. When ready to fish, he grasps each of his two birds in turn, tying rice straw around its neck to prevent it from swallowing the catch completely. Unleashed from the raft, the cormorant enters the water and dives from the surface. Once submerged, webbed feet propel the bird through the water. It surfaces momentarily to breathe, a thrashing fish clutched in its powerful hooked bill. Making repeated dives, the cormorant readjusts its hold so that the fish is partially swallowed, head first.

<< Lit by his lamp as dawn breaks, a cormorant fisherman crouches on his bamboo raft with his birds.

^ A trained cormorant surfaces with a live carp in its powerful hooked bill. Here is an example of the tripartite association between a human, a predator and its prey, similar to the way Kazakh herdsman train golden eagles to hunt corsac foxes.

> Starting to make a fisherman's traditional bamboo hat.

With the bounty safely grasped in the cormorant's bill, the fisherman dips a bamboo pole into the water for the bird to climb out, then swings it round on to the raft. He extracts the fish from the cormorant's grasp and drops it in the basket. After amassing six fish, he unties the ligature so that the bird is rewarded with the next fish it catches. To prevent the birds wasting time fighting over a fish, they are unleashed one at a time.

Local people also use nets to catch fish and shrimps from the Yangshuo River. As well as carp there are eels and mandarin fish (*Siniperca chuatsi*). This stalking predator thrives in rivers rich in water weeds, feeding solely on the fry of other fish. Chinese grass carp (*Ctenopharyngodon idellus*) are reared in carp ponds, where they are fed on submerged aquatic plants that are collected from the shallow river either by wading or, in warmer weather, by diving down. Either way, the plants are heaped onto a bamboo raft which is paddled ashore. From here, they are transported in a vehicle before the final leg of the journey, when they are piled up on carriers hung from a yoke so that the fishermen can take them along a raised path bordering a rice paddy or field to the carp pond.

Carp culture originated along the Yangtze at least as long ago as 475 BC and possibly earlier – this is the date when the earliest monograph of fish culture was written. By the time of the Tang Dynasty (AD 618–904), the common carp (*Cyprinus carpio*) was widely cultivated. During this period, the Emperor had the family name of Li, which also happened to be the carp's common name; this led to an imperial decree prohibiting the culture and sale of common carp. By then, the Chinese fish farmers were so preoccupied with fish culture it did not take them long to realise that silver carp (*Hypophthalmichthys molitrix*), bighead carp (*Hypophthalmichthys nobilis*), grass carp and mud carp (*Cirrhinus chinensis*) could all be reared in ponds. They also discovered that, because each species lives at a different level, feeding on a distinct diet, all four could be kept in a single suitable pond – a practice known as polyculture. Far from the royal decree being a disaster for the fish farmers, it turned out to be a blessing in disguise for the development of aquaculture.

A native of China, the grass carp can be found from the Pearl River in the south up to the Heilongjiang or Amur River that forms the border with the Russian Far East, from where it gets its alternative name of white amur. This fish has been introduced to over 40 countries, either as a food source or to keep aquatic vegetation in check; it was introduced to the United States in 1963 specifically to reduce vigorous waterweeds. However, care has to be taken with grass carp populations: if they reach high densities these fish have the potential to remove *all* the weeds from an aquatic system. Quite apart from the aesthetic value of aquatic plants in lakes, they are an essential part of a viable food chain.

⌐ Herbivorous Chinese grass carp or white amur have been imported to many countries to keep aquatic plants in check and as a source of food.

∧ A fisherman carries aquatic plants on a yoke to feed carp in Yangshuo.

< Aquatic plants collected from Yulong River near Dragon Bridge are piled up on a bamboo raft, ready to feed cultivated grass carp.

101

Carp are popular subjects in both Chinese ink-brush paintings and coloured-ink paintings, where ornamental fish are often depicted swimming amongst lotus lilies. They also brought dynamic colour to Chinese classical gardens. Today, few parks and public gardens in China are without a large pond filled with brightly coloured carp that visitors love to feed. Indeed, it was the Chinese who first reared carp as ornamental fish. After they refined their techniques for breeding carp for food, they began to select goldfish for their colour. Goldfish share a common ancestry with the crucian carp (*Carassius carassius*) and are bred for their body shape and colour. Koi carp, on the other hand,

have developed from common carp and were first bred in the 1820s in Japan – long after the Chinese began breeding goldfish. Koi are larger than goldfish and are reared for their colours and patterns, notably when viewed from above as they swim in the water below.

Also living in the rivers around Yangshuo are the alien South American apple snails (*Pomacea* sp.). These have invaded many countries and I was dismayed to see their tell-tale gum-pink eggs plastered over the rocks in the receding waters of the Jinbao River. They can survive becoming exposed, but they must be kept damp. In some natural wetlands these snails have been known to munch their way through 95 per cent of the

^ Ornamental koi carp jostle for food at a lake surface in Kunming.

< Two alien species: the gum-pink eggs of the South American apple snail laid on water hyacinth leaves in the Jinbao River.

ˇ A Yangshuo farmer still uses the traditional method of ploughing his rice fields with a water buffalo.

aquatic vegetation. Looking out towards the middle of the river I spotted more eggs, laid on another species originating in South America – the water hyacinth (*Eichhornia crassipes*). Given optimum growing conditions, this vigorous plant can double its population in two weeks, forming a floating platform that cuts out light reaching submerged aquatic plants and other life.

Yangshuo farmers still plough rice paddies using water buffalo; after working in the fields, the buffalo enjoy bathing and swimming in the river and may be seen lounging in the water. You can often spot them during a river cruise or when cycling along the minor roads that reach the riverbank.

Karst landscapes may not offer such a broad spectrum of plants and wildlife as natural forests, but they certainly arrest attention and will continue to inspire artists to portray them in a range of media for centuries to come.

CHAPTER 7

FOLLOWING THE PLANT HUNTERS

It had been a dismal drive up towards the lake Kangding Xian Cuo, through rain and then low clouds, but on rounding a corner we encountered gently sloping ground crisscrossed with bifurcating shallow streams flowing down around raised hummocks. The most conspicuous plants were the stately Alexander rhubarb, whose large, semi-translucent bracts hide the tiny flowers and protect them by sheltering them from the elements and by absorbing ultraviolet radiation. Growing alongside the rhubarb was a dwarf rhododendron with pale mauve flowers emerging from small silvery leaves.

< Stately spikes of Alexander rhubarb (*Rheum alexandrae*) with *Rhododendron impeditum* in a wet valley at 3,820 m (12,500 ft), near Kangding Xian Cuo.

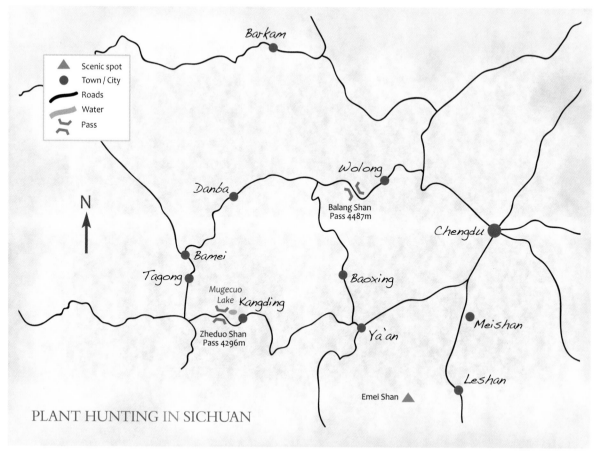

PLANT HUNTING IN SICHUAN

June and July are the prime months to explore the high meadows of Yunnan and Sichuan for a glorious array of alpines. It was these two provinces in particular that in the 19th and early 20th centuries attracted plant hunters – notably E. H. Wilson (who introduced over one thousand plants to the West and became known as 'Chinese' Wilson), Reginald Farrer and Joseph Rock, as well as the French missionaries Père David and Jean Marie Delavay – to seek out bountiful botanical treasures. In addition to alpine and herbaceous plants they also collected rhododendrons, magnolias and camellias, most of which flower earlier in the year, although diminutive high-altitude rhododendrons do bloom in the summer. All these plants have enriched Western gardens.

Towards the end of June, my husband Martin and I joined a small group on a plant-hunting trip to Sichuan. We arrived at the height of the swine-flu alert and had to remain seated on the plane until medics arrived dressed in biohazard gear to record the temperature of our foreheads. We sat there with our fingers crossed, knowing our fate for the next few days depended on the outcome. If we – or anyone in our row or three rows in front or behind us – had a high temperature, we would end up in quarantine for a week.

Fortunately, we escaped that scenario and set out from Chengdu in three four-wheel-drive vehicles. Our initial destination was Wolong, a World Heritage Site located high in the mountains of Sichuan, best known as China's flagship panda reserve (see Chapter 4).

We were aware that this area lay close to the epicentre of the 12 May 2008 earthquake and that the road up the valley was not in good condition, but we were encouraged

< A buff-tip moth (*Phalera* sp.) mimics a broken birch twig at Wolong.

^ Apart from insects, wildlife is not abundant on alpine turf or scrub. But not far from Zhedou Shan Pass, near a wet patch of ground, we found this frog beside gentians in flower.

> Yellow lampshade poppy or yellow poppywort (*Meconopsis integrifolia*) after rain. This plant was collected by E. H. Wilson on his second plant-hunting trip to China, 1903–1905.

>> *Thalictrum delavayi* flowers beside the Sha Chung river valley near Danba show the male phase, below, with stamens hanging down, and the female phase, above, after the stamens have fallen to expose the stigmas.

to discover a new expressway to the Min River. When we emerged from a tunnel, however, the devastation was all too apparent – brown gashes punctuated the green-clothed peaks where vast landslides had plucked off all the vegetation. The steep mountains are particularly susceptible to landslides during earthquakes, because active seismic faults cut through the region where the flat terrain of the Sichuan Basin meets the mountainous eastern edge of the Tibetan Plateau.

^ A vigorous rose in flower beside the Wolong road near our hotel.

v *Corydalis flexuosa* is a striking fumewort found along the lower part of the road from Wolong to Balang Shan, at around 2,000 m (6,500 ft).

On leaving the expressway we wriggled our way around the road diggers, looking in vain for Sargent's lily (*Lilium sargentiae*), named after the wife of Charles Sprague Sargent (1841–1927), the director of the Arnold Arboretum at Harvard. But the whole area had been completely buried by a landslip. After some single-lane dirt tracks we found the start of the steep-sided Wolong road that follows the Pitiao River, which feeds into the Min. Building after building was in ruins. In places we drove through thick dust clouds; elsewhere we saw how fallen rocks had dammed the river to form lakes in which small boats were anchored.

Compared to the many trips I had made to Wolong in the past, the traffic was sparse – the abysmal condition of the road would deter any faint-hearted traveller, and travel agents had been discouraged from sending groups here because the accommodation was so limited after the earthquake. For me, the most shattering experience was seeing the Wolong Hotel, where I had stayed many times,

<< Mountain flowers in the mist: yellow *Caltha palustris* (a variety of the marsh marigold), purple *Omphalogramma vincaeflora* and pink *Primula nutans* near Balang Shan Pass.

< A lousewort on the road to Barkam lives as a partial parasite on grasses and has a beak in a contrasting colour to the rest of the flower. These flowers are pollinated by bumblebees vibrating their flight muscles, which releases the pollen – a process known as buzz-pollination.

reduced to a pile of rubble. Instead, we were lodged in a newly built wooden block at the Muwu Hotel, where the bathroom was three in one – an open-plan room with an Asian toilet in the floor, a basin and an unenclosed shower.

Wolong is rightly renowned as the largest and most important of all the 60-plus giant panda reserves in China, but this highly biodiverse area, which ranges from 1,200 to 6,250 m (4,000–20,500 ft) in altitude, is also home to copious mammals, an extensive bird list and a staggering 4,000 species of plants. Most people live and farm along the river valleys, which they cross either on zip wires or on swaying cable bridges. At the lower levels lush deciduous and evergreen temperate forests, together with bamboo groves, clothe the slopes. Higher up, conifers appear: these form the high-altitude forests. Above the tree line are the high alpine meadows where alpines flourish and yak graze. Finally, there are some 20 glacier-covered mountain peaks.

Many roadside plants living in the 1,000–2,500 m (3,000–8,000 ft) belt are types familiar to anyone who gardens in a temperate climate. Roses and clematis scramble over shrubs and smaller trees; willows, maples and rhododendrons intermingle with bamboos. Within the herb layer beneath the trees are anemones, geraniums, violets and orchids, while in wetter areas drifts of iris flourish. In more sheltered spots in forest glades the elegant, understated *Paris polyphylla* was blooming.

It was a delight to see again the intense blue fumewort *Corydalis flexuosa* flowering out in the open. The range of *Corydalis* species in Sichuan is amazing. We were a little too early to see the newly described *C. panda* from Balang Shan, but each day we came across species we had not seen before, in an array of colour combinations ranging from yellow flowers with blue tips to white with black markings. Louseworts (*Pedicularis* spp.), also in a variety of colour mixes, were prominent, especially in wetter patches.

< Nodding *Lilium lophophorum* flowers resemble miniature lanterns, with the petal-like tepals fused at their tips. This helps to protect the inner floral parts from severe weather; yet open slits ensure insects can enter to pollinate the flowers. This curious lily was first collected by the French explorer Prince Henri d'Orléans in 1890.

∧ These low-growing slipper orchids add to the kaleidoscope of colours punctuating the alpine pasture on Balang Shan.

>> My first sighting of a red poppywort had petals that looked like crunched red tissue paper, with raindrops decorating the hairy stems.

∨ Red poppywort petals bent back to show the white stamens.

Each of us had our own particular prime targets. Top of my list was the beautiful red poppywort (*Meconopsis punicea*), known in China as *hong hua lu rong hao*; its pendulous red petals resemble miniature prayer flags flapping in the breeze. I had seen it in flower at Kew Gardens years ago and knew it grew in damp alpine meadows, often with other lampshade poppies. In areas which are heavily grazed by yak, the plants tend to be confined to low scrub, from which the flowers emerge, but in ungrazed areas extensive patches occur. The icing on the cake was seeing their hairy stems festooned with raindrops that glistened like diamonds.

In 1903, E. H. Wilson travelled almost 1,000 km (600 miles), from Kangding to Kangali Pass north of Songpan, to collect seed of this striking plant, guided by a scrap of

information on a specimen label in Kew Herbarium. It was introduced to cultivation in the West several times, but had been lost for some 25 years before being reintroduced in 1986 by Peter Cox and Peter Hutchison after one of their many Chinese seed-collecting expeditions. Almost every flower I examined had several flies foraging inside; outside China insect pollination is unreliable, so the flowers have to be pollinated by hand and the seeds germinate only after they are subjected to frost.

Growing alongside the poppyworts, the deep purple flowers of *Omphalogramma vincaeflora* resembled outsized butterworts and the dark red slipper orchids (*Cypripedium tibeticum*) with their inflated purple-red 'slippers' added to the kaleidoscope of colours punctuating the grassy meadows.

< The orange Père David's lily is one of several striking lilies in the Sha Chung river valley near Danba at 2,500 m (8,200 ft).

ᵛ Magnificent regal lilies flower on cliffs near Maoxian in the Min Valley. A green predatory spider lurks in wait for an unsuspecting insect pollinator.

Once we had our eye in for lilies that emerged from cracks in roadside rock faces and cascaded down towards the road, we found them in several places and the safest way to photograph them was from below with a long telephoto lens. Thanks to Wilson, the regal lily (*Lilium regale*) graces many a herbaceous border in English country gardens. In Sichuan, atop the 1–1.5 m (3–5 ft) stem bearing slender leaves, impressive white trumpets begin to open in late June to early July. Wilson discovered this handsome

< This turk's cap lily with a dark bud was also found in the Sha Chung river valley near Danba.

∨ Sargent's lily, ending in glorious trumpet-shaped flowers, cascades down a vertical rock face near Baoxing.

plant in 1903 in the Min Valley and it was there that we began to spot the funnel-shaped flowers, often growing at a horizontal angle from rocky crevices high above the road. By this time, after we had been held up by repeated roadblocks, the light was fading fast, so we decided to press on to Maoxian. In better light the following morning, we found many blooms only a few minutes' drive up the valley from our hotel. Access with a tripod and camera up a steep slope covered with loose rocks was difficult, but worth the effort for the fragrant smell and to see a hoverfly linger to feast on the copious pollen.

Wilson collected thousands of regal lily bulbs from the Min Valley in 1908, but by the time they reached the Arnold Arboretum several months later they were all rotten. He returned to collect more, making sure this time that each bulb was coated in clay. The story of how a landslip descended onto the path along which he and his porters were travelling is well documented. Seeing the devastation wrought by the 2008 earthquake, we realised how lucky Wilson had been to escape with a broken leg. His tripod proved invaluable as a splint to support him on the journey down the mountain and for ever afterwards he walked with what he called his 'lily limp'.

We finally found Sargent's lily growing from a rock face beside the road not far outside Boaxian. Wilson discovered that these flowers are eaten in China like preserved cabbage: they are boiled and dried in the sun,

then minced and fried with salt and oil. Along the track that follows the Sha Chung river valley near Danba were two more choice lilies – the orange-flowered *Lilium davidii*, collected by Père David, and the crimson-flecked Turk's cap lily (*Lilium duchartrei*). This proved to be a very fruitful stretch for plant hunting, with the striking yellow flower spikes of Chinese golden raintrees (*Koelreuteria paniculata*) standing out amongst the green mantle.

In wet flushes and beside streams, an array of primulas comes into its own, including the pendulous yellow-flowered Himalayan cowslip (*P. sikkimensis*) and the deep purple *P. secundiflora*. In some places they form glorious floriferous carpets. Also favouring wetter areas are the stately spikes of yellow-flowered *Cremanthodium brunneopilosum*; with long narrow petals they are easily spotted from a vehicle when growing in roadside pastures. This striking plant is rarely seen in cultivation.

On the road to Barkam we came across a yak round-up where several hundred animals were corralled for

∧ The striking *Cremanthodium brunneopilosum* grows in a wet meadow on the road from Barkam to Ruo Er Gai at 3,350 m (11,000 ft).

> Two primulas – yellow Himalayan cowslips (*P. sikkimensis*) and purple *P. secundiflora* – with a crucifer in flower beside a stream at Kangding Mugecuo Scenic Area.

horn-branding, ear-tagging and hair-cutting. To avoid any risk of their being trampled underfoot, the calves had been separated from the adults and left outside the fenced area. Many Tibetan families live in the western part of Sichuan that abuts the Tibet Special Administrative Region (SAR). Yak provide them with milk, butter, candles and meat; the long hair is made into ropes and the soft downy hair, shed annually, is spun into cloth or made into felt for their dark tents or yurts. Too dense a population of yak, however, tends to have an adverse effect on the high-alpine flora, because the ground gets trampled and overgrazed,

so that inevitably some flowers are eaten.

Travelling south-west from Chengdu on the Sichuan–Tibet highway, you come to the mountain town of Kangding. Squeezed into a valley on either side of the Zheduo River, which races through the centre, Kangding has long been an important staging post on the way to Lhasa. For centuries, yak hides and wool, Tibetan herbs and tea bricks from Ya'an have been traded here between Chinese and Tibetans. Today Kangding is best known for the Kangding Love Song extolling the beauty of Paoma Shan, which towers above the town.

Things can change quickly in China. In less than a year since our group leader had last visited, a quiet mountain road up to an area with alpine pastures, lake and hot springs had been transformed with a huge car park at the entrance and was now being marketed as the Kangding Mugecuo Scenic Area. Here you board one of the obligatory tour buses that takes you up the new tarmac road to the lake. Each bus has a video screen showing highlights of the area with music blaring out, but it was worth enduring for the plants within the forest and on alpine pastures.

Strips of primulas lined the stream banks and beard lichens festooned the conifers on the walk up to an open grassy area grazed by horses kept to hire out to tourists. The most obvious flowers were outsized deep pink *Incarvillea compacta*, typically appearing on short stems. Many were partially hidden beneath scrub where they had survived being munched by the horses.

Another trip out from Kangding was to Kangding Xian Cuo, a high-altitude lake at 4,000 m (13,000 ft). Just below it, where shallow water flows over stony ground, were impressive stands of Alexander rhubarb (*Rheum alexandrae*), an ornamental relative of edible rhubarb. By the time we reached the lake we were enveloped in cloud, but the yellow *Meconopsis integrifolia* and blue *M. lancifolia* flowers shone through the mist.

On the way down we stopped beside a patch of the extensive wind-pruned forest where the high-altitude *Rhododendron phaeochrysum* had been chopped down for fuel, leaving the ground beneath exposed.

< An exquisite lichen carpet on fallen *Rhododendron phaeochrysum* leaves. This miniature fairyland was exposed after the woody shrubs had been cut for fuel, below Kangding Xian Cuo.

∧ *Incarvillea compacta* grows on grassland near Zhedou Shan Pass.

⌐ Children delight in picking *Incarvillea* flowers to use as ephemeral kazoos.

> A sea of prayer flags with a chorten (Buddhist shrine) behind, at the 5,100m (16,700 ft) high Zhedou Shan Pass.

The evergreen rhododendrons would have cut out most of the light, so it was no surprise that flowering plants were absent; instead an exquisite lichen ground flora was flourishing on a spongy rhododendron-leaf compost. Now exposed to the elements and direct light, this patch of shade-loving lichens was doomed.

Later on we passed the newly opened Kangding Airport, built at an altitude of 4,280 metres (14,000 ft) – higher than Lhasa. With Chengdu a mere 35-minute flight away, instead of six hours by road, this now provides easy access to the Mugecuo Scenic Area and even a day trip becomes possible.

We had planned to visit the first great meander of the Yellow River as it enters China from Tibet and then drive to Rua Er Gai for the night, but we were halted at a checkpoint manned by traffic police, with the army much in evidence. All vehicles carrying Chinese people were waved through and, when we queried this, the familiar phrase 'For your own safety' was trotted out. We guessed the real reason was that the authorities wanted to avoid our being in contact with an area of unrest close to the Tibetan border. We had no option but to turn back. We found a small hotel, but no sooner had we booked in than we had a message to say the police insisted we drive back to a bigger town, because the hotel we had chosen allegedly did not have a permit for foreign visitors. When we checked in at Hong Yuan we discovered – rather spookily – that the police had already made a reservation for us! This is the only time in all my travels to China, spanning 25 years, that I have been prevented from going somewhere.

In high-altitude turf areas in Sichuan a curious and lucrative insect/fungus association occurs. If caterpillars become infected with the spores of the caterpillar fungus *Cordyceps sinensis*, the parasite permeates the caterpillar tissues to produce a club-shaped spore body that emerges from the turf. The two are collected intact and sold in bundles. For over 2,000 years, this combination has been used in TCM as a tonic and an aphrodisiac. It is thought to reduce fatigue, to lower cholesterol levels and to have anti-ageing and anti-oxidant properties. More recently, since being marketed as a natural substitute for Viagra, it has fetched such high prices that turf wars take place over the best collecting areas, resulting in 13 people being killed during 2008 in south Sichuan alone.

Discovering orchids is always a bonus. Having had our appetite whetted between Wolong and Balang Shan Pass, with *Calanthe tricarinata* in wooded areas and the Tibetan *Cypripedium* on higher grassland, we were eager to find others. A book on local orchids in

^ *Calanthe tricarinata* orchid flowers at the entrance to Dasheng Valley, above Wolong. The flowers have lime-green tepals and a frilled red lip.

> The tiny pink flowers of a ladies' tresses orchid (*Spiranthes sinensis*) grow in a spiral around the stem.

the Huanglong Visitor Centre showed the pink flowers of a ladies' tresses orchid (*Spiranthes sinensis*) in July. Like the Eurasian *S. autumnalis*, the flowers are arranged spirally on the stem. We had almost given up hope of finding this gem when we drove through Danyun Gorge to Fengping village, where some local children picked a bunch of flowers to present to our group. It contained a single spike of the *Spiranthes*, but when we asked them to show us where they had found it, they took us to a barren piece of ground – sadly, they had picked the one and only flower!

Sichuan proved to be a very rewarding experience and I have mentioned only a small fraction of the plants we found. We had the advantage of following in the footsteps of famed plant hunters, in areas where botanists have worked since the exploratory trips, so we were well prepared with plant lists. Nonetheless, the thrill of the hunt was with us each day, because getting the timing right is just as crucial as knowing the best locations for any successful botanical trip.

CHAPTER 8

A TROPICAL PARADISE

We had been watching a white-cheeked gibbon foraging on leaves high up in the canopy all afternoon. For most of the time, the views were of a nondescript honey-coloured furry mass, but occasionally as she moved through the treetops we glimpsed a long arm reaching out for a branch or legs dangling as she swung. After several hours of craning our necks we were rewarded with our first good view of a tiny baby clinging to its mother's belly like glue. Also honey-coloured, it was just 14 days old, with spidery arms and legs. When the mother stood or sat on a branch, the baby let go with one arm and turned its head to reveal a tiny black face.

< A mother northern white-cheeked gibbon pauses on a branch with her two-week-old baby, which clings to her from the moment it is born. Loss of habitat has reduced populations of this charismatic ape to a critically endangered level.

121

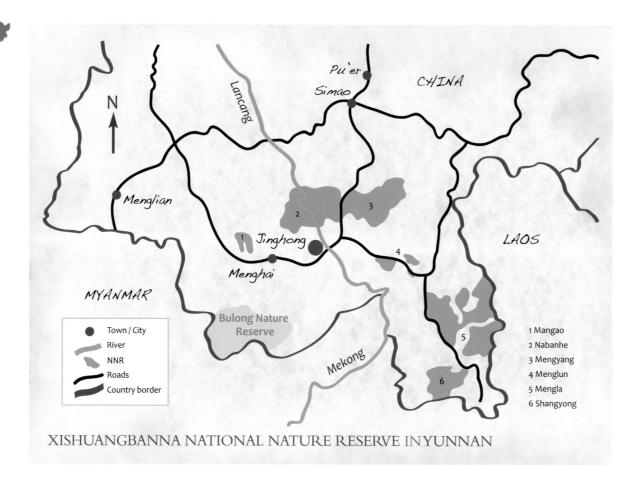

Town / City
River
NNR
Roads
Country border

1 Mangao
2 Nabanhe
3 Mengyang
4 Menglun
5 Mengla
6 Shangyong

XISHUANGBANNA NATIONAL NATURE RESERVE IN YUNNAN

Yunnan province is divided, from north to south, into three climatic zones – temperate, sub-tropical and tropical – each supporting varied habitats with an array of plants. Indeed, this province is known as the kingdom of plants: of the 30,000 species in China, more than half occur in Yunnan. The southern part, which borders onto Myanmar, Laos and Vietnam, lies just south of the Tropic of Cancer, at the northern edge of South-East Asia's tropical zone.

It is the topography of the far south that has created essential conditions for a flourishing rainforest environment. Mountain ranges to the north prevent cold, damp air from flowing south, and monsoons that blow in from the south-west and south-east are funnelled into the central region by mountains to the west and east. As the warm, humid air reaches the mountains, it condenses to produce abundant rain during the wet season (May to October), when temperatures are high. November to April is the dry season, but early-morning fog helps to maintain the humidity within the rainforest. The result is a semi-humid monsoon tropical climate with an annual rainfall ranging from 1,200 to 2,500 mm (47–98 in).

The rainforest area was once much more extensive, but agriculture, development, new roads and rubber plantations have all encroached on this rich habitat. Satellite images show that the forest cover in general was reduced by almost 20 per cent between 1976 and 2003. The remaining rainforest is now fragmented, but five distinct areas are embraced within the Xishuangbanna NNR. Even though it covers a mere 0.2 per cent of China's landmass, the reserve contains a vast range of plant species: 6 per cent of all those found in China. These in turn support a rich and varied fauna, with flowers providing nectar and pollen for insects – notably spectacular butterflies – and smaller birds, while arboreal species such as birds, bats, monkeys and squirrels fly in or climb up to feast on the fruits.

^ Sunlight bathes shrubs, trees and lianas within the Wild Elephant Valley rainforest.

< A blue tiger butterfly (*Tirumala limniace*) sips nectar from a lantana flower.

<< Flowers of trees such as these Buddhist bauhinia (*Bauhinia variegata*) are enjoyed by monkeys and collected as an ingredient for stir-fry dishes in Yunnan, where banana flowers are also eaten.

123

The largest of the six reserves within Xishuangbanna is Mengyang, where access to most areas is restricted. But one small part, known as Yexianggu or Wild Elephant Valley – so named from a small group of Asian elephants (*Elephas maximus*) which move up from Laos to feed and drink – is a commercial enterprise run for tourists. Lying only 29 km (18 miles) away from Jinghong on the highway, this is an easy location to visit. Groups begin to arrive at 8 a.m., each accompanied by a guide using a megaphone. Fortunately they soon depart to see the elephant and ethnic shows, leaving few people, apart from the rangers, in the forest itself. So I decided to spend several days with Sam Yan Zhuang, who had guided me here in 2007. On this, my third trip to Wild Elephant Valley, I had high hopes of seeing my target species – the Asian elephant.

Part of the trail is along a raised walkway, which gives an elevated view of the forest and allows elephants to walk beneath it. They come to drink in the Sancha River, where remnants of the original wooden tree houses remain in the forks of a few trees. In their heyday, the tree houses provided scientists and tourists with a better and safer view of the elephants: in this romantic setting, the sounds of the forest could be absorbed throughout the day and night. After the houses were deemed no longer safe, several decidedly unromantic and very basic concrete rooms were built on elevated posts. In 2007, I stayed in one of these, but two years later they were all closed after elephants damaged some of their supports; so this time I had to stay in a bungalow built on a slope near the entrance to the reserve and commute to the forest each day. My spacious room was surprisingly cold at night, so I was glad an electric blanket was provided.

< A twisted woody liana hangs down over the path from an overhead tree.

∨ The torch ginger (*Etlingera elatior*) flower is so named because it resembles a flaming torch: single flowers appear on their own stems beneath tall leaves. Also known in Yunnan as the China rose, it is now cultivated as a tropical ornamental and possibly naturalised in forests at lower elevations.

To reduce the risk of encountering an elephant, visitors are not allowed to walk the trails between 6 p.m. and 8 a.m., so for a speedy ascent into the forest I opted for a ride in the first cable car of the day. With the mist still lingering, we had some atmospheric aerial views of the forest below. Indeed, this viewpoint is perfect for appreciating the varied heights of the upper forest layer, where many trees are covered with a lush green blanket of creepers. The giants of the forest are supported by huge buttress roots spreading out from their trunks, while many figs have copious aerial roots that descend from above and take root when they reach the ground. All the vegetation was dripping with water condensed from the mist, which also revealed copious spiders' webs.

On one journey we were serenaded by melodious music emanating from the cab behind us with some ethnic minority youngsters – a boy playing his *hulusi* (a musical instrument made from a gourd and bamboo stems) accompanied by girls singing a Dai song. The Dai people, one of ten minorities that inhabit the region, have learnt how to live in harmony with the rainforest by utilising natural resources in such a way that they are maintained, not destroyed. They even plant fuel wood around their villages so as not to destroy the native trees.

^ The gaudy male Mrs Gould's sunbird (*Aethopyga gouldiae*) is much more conspicuous than its drab mate. Sunbirds fill the niche that is occupied in the New World by hummingbirds, flitting from one flower to another and probing inside with their slender bill so that the long tongue can sip the nectar.

ᵛ Bamboo looms out of the mist in an early morning view from the cable car above Wild Elephant Valley.

125

The green peafowl has metallic green neck feathers which vary in colour depending on the angle of the light, with a distinct patch of bare yellow skin beneath the eyes. Known as dragonbirds in China, peafowl often feature as ornaments on Dai houses. To the Dai people, the green peacock is a symbol of peace, happiness and good fortune.

Sam had heard via the grapevine that the female of a pair of semi-wild northern white-cheeked gibbons (*Nomascus leucogenys*) had recently been seen in the forest with her newborn baby. So on walking down from the cable-car station we quizzed one of the forest rangers, but no one had yet seen or heard any gibbons that day.

As you set off along the trails inside the rainforest, the lower layers are immediately obvious. Green remains the dominant colour, with each kind of plant having its own niche for gaining the optimum amount of light to enable it to grow, flower and set seed. Herbaceous plants, including an array of gingers whose ornamental flowers were fading in December, give way to shrubs of various sizes interspersed with bamboos, wild bananas and smaller trees. In their race for the light, creepers climb and entwine, while vines and woody-stemmed lianas crisscross branches as they scramble up and over them.

Against this green backcloth multi-coloured birds such as bee-eaters, sunbirds and minivets flit in and out to feast on the array of flowers that appear at different times of the year. Larger birds include hornbills and various parrots. Green peafowl (*Pavo muticus*) feed on seeds, grasses, flowers, fallen fruits such as figs, and even insects.

A glance upwards reveals an impressive hanging garden of plants that live perched on the branches and within the forks of higher trees. These epiphytes include bird's nest

^ A cloud of tadpoles in the Sancha River sticks together in a group: safety in numbers is a useful anti-predator device.

< The epiphytic orchid *Dendrobium aphyllum* produces copious fragrant flowers on pendulous leafless canes that cascade from the branches of rainforest trees in April.

ᵛ An Asian water monitor swims at dusk with its legs pressed against its body, which it moves in an S motion.

ferns (*Asplenium nidus*), several climbing aroids and many orchids, none of which have to compete for space on the ground. Summer is the best time to see the orchids in flower. Gaps in the overhead canopy are rare and largely confined to places where rivers flow or where large trees have crashed to the ground, when young saplings begin their race upwards to fill the gap.

We repeatedly heard frogs calling from beneath the riverbank, but never managed to glimpse any, although we did see a cloud of tadpoles swimming around as a fluid clump. Tributaries from the Mekong River (known in China as the Lancang) permeate the forest, where Asian monitor lizards (*Varanus salvator*) may be seen swimming and soft-shelled turtles basking on rocks or fallen trunks. Many of the fishes found here also occur in Vietnam, Laos, Myanmar and India; these include a number of small ornamental species such as danios, rasboras and gouramis, known to the tropical fish trade. At the other end of the scale is one of the fastest-growing fish in the world, the giant Mekong catfish (*Pangasianodon gigas*), which is capable of reaching 3 m (10 ft) in length and is endemic to the Mekong basin. A combination of overfishing and loss of habitat means that this piscatorial heavyweight is now classified as critically endangered.

^ A two-week-old white-cheeked gibbon clings to its mother as she hangs by both hands from an overhead branch.

We heard the gibbons before we saw them. The full-throated duet of an adult pair is an evocative, haunting sound that permeates the forest early in the morning. These natural gymnasts use their ridiculously long arms (so long that the lower part has to be held curved upwards to avoid it hitting the ground on the rare occasions when the animals descend from the trees to walk) to swing from one branch to another, with the four fingers curled around a branch like a hook. They are highly skilled at moving through the canopy, covering as much as 12 m (40 ft) horizontally and even more when they drop down from one branch to another in a single swing. Should a gibbon grasp a rotten branch that breaks free, it simply falls a bit further until another branch is within grasping distance. When the gibbons move at speed through the canopy, it is impossible to focus the camera, but periodically they pause either to feed or for a grooming session. Then they may use any combination of arms and legs to move at a more leisurely pace from one branch to another – sometimes even walking upright along a branch, holding their arms up to balance themselves like tightrope walkers.

Investing a lot of time over many days gazing up into the canopy paid off, for I was rewarded with several good sightings of the mother gibbon with her newborn baby. Young northern white-cheeked gibbons and adult males are jet black with white cheek tufts and a black head tuft, whereas the females are an attractive golden colour with black eye patches. Babies are also golden for the first six months, after which both sexes turn black; then, as a female matures, she reverts to developing golden fur. Virtually as soon as it is born, a baby starts to cling to its mother's fur with long fingers and toes. Only when the mother rests on a branch to feed on leaves, flowers or fruits does the youngster release its grip with one hand and turn its head to absorb the surroundings.

The northern white-cheeked gibbon occurs from southern Yunnan into northern Laos and northern Vietnam and is listed as critically endangered. In the 1960s, some 1,000 individuals were estimated to be living in China; two decades later, the population had plummeted to 100. In December 2008 Drs Fan Peng-Fei and Huo Sheng made a short interview survey within villages close to where the gibbons used to live. After discovering that few people could remember hearing wild gibbons calling, they concluded that the monkeys were probably on the verge of extinction in China.

^ The mother gibbon hangs with one hand as she prepares to swing through the canopy with her tiny baby.

⌐ The extraordinarily long arms of one male white-cheeked gibbon are visible as he pauses between lianas early in the morning.

> A male northern white-cheeked gibbon in the Wild Elephant Valley rainforest displays his conspicuous white cheek patches.

It would be hard to find a greater contrast between the speed at which a gibbon flies through the canopy by day and the rate at which a slow loris moves around at night. The Bengal slow loris (*Nycticebus bengalensis*) is one of several species that live in South-East Asia and China. Their fluffy bodies and large round eyes make these mammals highly desirable as cute pets. Slow lorises are also eaten in China and their bones are used for TCM. These factors, together with fragmentation and loss of habitats cleared for planting cash crops such as rubber, sugar cane and coffee, mean they are now vulnerable.

During the day, slow lorises sleep off the ground in the branches of a tree or in a tree hole; they curl themselves up into a tight ball, with their heads between their thighs. Only after the sun has set do they become active and descend to drink – and to feed, if no prey is found in the sleeping tree. The slow loris is an opportunistic carnivore, eating insects, snails, eggs and even lizards and small birds if it can catch them. It creeps up on its prey, making a quick snatch with both hands. If prey is not found, the slow loris will eat fruits, leaves or gum oozing from tree bark.

Slow lorises do not have the option of making a hasty retreat from their predators; instead they use a toxin produced from glands on the insides of their elbows mixed with saliva as a protection against enemies. Mothers even coat their offspring by licking their fur before leaving them to go in search of food. If the toxin fails to deter a predator, the slow loris can drop to the ground and roll up into a protective ball.

< By day, the slow loris remains largely hidden amongst branches as a curled-up ball of fur. As soon as the sun sets, it wakes up and uncurls to reveal a round head with a white strip between the outsized eyes surrounded by a dark eye ring.

> Oak leaf butterflies resemble dry leaves as they rest on a tree trunk. Some feed on the sap early in the morning.

⬎ These cluster-tree fig (*Ficus racemosa*) fruits grow directly from the woody trunk and are a popular food for a host of forest animals, from squirrels and monkeys to birds.

∨ Typical of nocturnal mammals, a slow loris has large eyes whose pupils contract during the day. The felling of their sleeping and feeding trees in Xishuangbanna rainforest has led to a decline in slow loris populations.

131

<< Rhesus macaques live in mixed male and female troops and move through the rainforest to forage on flowers, fruits, leaves, buds and seeds; they also turn over stones in rivers, searching for aquatic invertebrates and fish. Youngsters enjoy chasing one another up and down trees or simply swinging from a branch.

< Pouch-like cheeks enable rhesus macaques to gather food quickly, temporarily hoarding it in the pouches. The monkeys can then move to safer surroundings to spend time chewing and swallowing their food.

Another forest primate is the rhesus macaque (*Macaca mulatta*) – the most studied of any non-human primate in the field of biomedical research. This species is like a slimmed-down version of the Tibetan macaque, with a longer tail and without the hairy face; it also moves around on all fours both on the ground and up in trees. Rhesus macaques are omnivores and feed on a wide array of plants and invertebrates such as termites, grasshoppers and beetles, as well as fungi, birds' eggs, fish and fruits. Habitat destruction is not such a problem with these primates because they adapt well to living in close association with humans; indeed, they will frequently raid crops and forage through garbage. However, they can become pests and, once people feel threatened, they will retaliate by stoning, shooting or trapping them.

One of the easiest places to see a troop of rhesus macaques is in the Xishuangbanna Primeval Forest Park (Yuanshi Senlin Gongyuan), just 8 km (5 miles) east of Jinghong. This is not a nature reserve, but a highly commercialised area peppered with souvenir shops where busloads of tourists converge to view ethnic performances. There is a nature trail through a small but intact patch of old-growth rainforest where, once again, the peace is shattered by tour leaders with megaphones. However, most of the tourists leave by mid- to late afternoon and this is the time to take an electric cart to the top of the concrete road. The macaques begin to emerge from the forest and move down to the river just before being fed late in the afternoon.

Each day in Wild Elephant Valley we took a leisurely walk back to our rooms. One day we found an agitated middle-aged lady sitting beside the path. All she could tell Sam was her name and that she came from Mongolia. She could not remember the name of her guide or the tour company. Having felt a bit tired, she had sat down and lost contact with her group. We escorted her back to the car park where her son was greatly relieved to see her again, several hours after they had been separated. Jinghong's tropical climate attracts tourists from all over China – especially those living in the northern latitudes that are frigid in winter. As well as the congenial climate, the varied minority peoples and their way of life are a great attraction in this region.

ⱽ Red mucronata (*Balanophora harlandii*) is a curious flowering plant that resembles a fungus. Instead of growing from the ground, it lives as a parasite on the woody roots of a shrub or tree and is used medicinally as a tonic for boosting energy levels. The tiny white flowers are amongst the smallest known.

133

On my last morning in Wild Elephant Valley, a ranger told us a male elephant had been seen, which raised my hopes of an encounter, only for them to be dashed when no further sightings had been made by midday. Then I remembered reading in the recently opened Elephant Museum that there was an Asian Elephant Breeding Center not far away. After talking to Sam at some length, I learnt that several elephants were released into the forest to feed each day and was keen to investigate whether I could see them feeding. He was dubious I would be granted permission, but I decided it was worth the effort.

As we entered the gates of the newly built centre, we passed the Copulation Room and the Delivery Room and I learnt that the first captive-bred Asian elephant in China had been born here in 2007. After much discussion, it was agreed that I could photograph the elephants on their return to the centre. However, after further clarification, this turned out to mean as they walked back along the road. Eventually, I managed to get our intermediary contact to persuade the Dai keepers (who speak to the elephants in Thai) to allow me to accompany them into the forest. We trekked for a while before wading through a river and climbing up back into the forest. Then we homed in on the loud cracks produced by elephants breaking outsized bamboo culms. Keeping my distance behind the keepers, I saw

two large elephants feeding; then another two smaller animals came into view. So, at the eleventh hour, I was able to photograph my first Asian elephants – albeit not completely wild ones – feeding in a Chinese rainforest. I was also thankful not to have become a statistic, like an American tourist who was found unconscious in 2008 at dusk by a ranger, having been attacked and tossed by a wild elephant.

Neither plants nor animals recognise arbitrary political boundaries; yet larger animals such as elephants need plenty of space to roam for the best food and watering places. Just as I was leaving Jinghong in December 2009, it was encouraging to learn that China and Laos had signed an agreement to build a trans-frontier nature reserve to provide better protection not only for some 250 Asian elephants that migrate back and forth, but also for other endangered species in the area. Hopefully, this will help to curtail the illegal hunting of gibbons and other wildlife, enabling them once again to frequent forests on both sides of the border.

Over many years spent travelling the world, I have been fortunate to see some stunning landscapes and fascinating animal behaviour, but the tiny gibbon baby – so dependent on its mother in the high-rise layer of the forest – is one of those magical moments that will live with me forever.

<< Asian elephants moving through the rainforest in Xishuangbanna NNR to feed.

< By the end of the dry season in April the Sancha River has dropped to a low level. It is rare for elephants to migrate into China at this time.

ᵛ Both the underwings, seen here, and the upper wings of the plain tiger butterfly (*Danaus chrysippus*) show a distinct warning coloration, which signals to predators to leave them well alone. These and other butterflies come down to the ground to sip water from puddles after rain.

CHAPTER 9

CHINA'S MAJESTIC TIGERS

The tiger is the largest and most magnificent of all the big cats, with conspicuous black vertical stripes on a rusty-red body. The stripe pattern is unique to each individual. Out in the open, a tiger appears very conspicuous, but among vegetation the stripes help to disrupt the body outline and serve as effective camouflage. The largest and heaviest cat in the world is the Amur, Siberian or Manchurian tiger, which develops an extra-thick coat to enable it to survive the frigid winters.

< As two Amur tigers stand up to spar in winter, the white belly with dark stripes on one becomes visible.

137

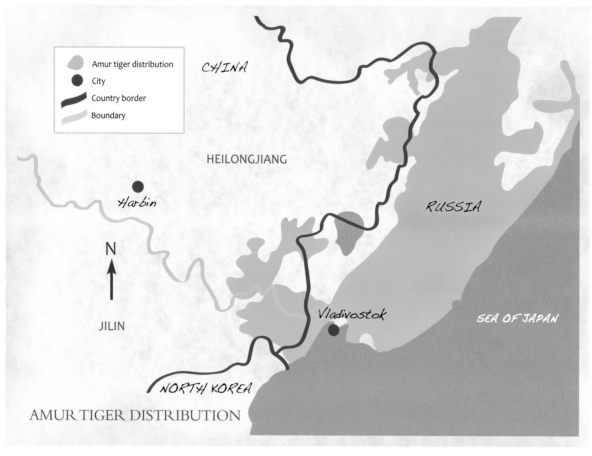

Amur tiger distribution
City
Country border
Boundary

CHINA

HEILONGJIANG

Harbin

N

JILIN

RUSSIA

Vladivostok

SEA OF JAPAN

NORTH KOREA

AMUR TIGER DISTRIBUTION

> Detail of an Amur tiger's winter coat, showing the long fluffy fur which helps to insulate the animal in severe weather.

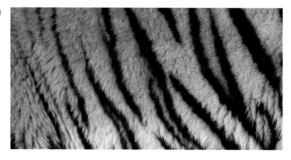

All tigers (*Panthera tigris*) originate from Asia, with nine subspecies being recognised; three of these are already extinct, while the rest are highly endangered and some are threatened with extinction. Tigers were once found all the way from Turkey in the west across to Siberia and Indonesia in the east; today they inhabit only 7 per cent of this area. Within the last century the world population of wild tigers has crashed by 95 per cent to somewhere between a minimum of 3,800 and a maximum of 5,180 in 2009. In addition, there are well over double that number of captive tigers languishing in zoos and tiger parks around the world. The major reasons for this plummeting decline are loss and fragmentation of habitat, logging, and hunting of tigers and of their prey species.

Wild tigers are counted either by remote camera traps triggered by a passing animal, which can be identified by its stripes, or, in the case of Amur tigers, by tracks left in the snow. Instead of a live tiger being darted to get a blood sample to analyse its DNA and hence its bloodline, this can now be done by examining droppings, without any risk to a tiger's health.

In China, wild tigers now live an even more precarious existence than giant pandas, with an estimated total of 37–50 of them in the whole country. There may be ten Indochinese tigers (*Panthera tigris corbetti*) still living in the south-west (they are also found

< An alert Amur tiger climbs onto a rock to gain a higher viewpoint.

˅ A tiger knot-tassel wall-hanging, given as New Year present in the Year of the Tiger.

in Cambodia, Laos, Myanmar, Thailand and Vietnam). One of the last remaining in China was killed and eaten in 2009 in the far south of Yunnan; the culprit was given a 12-year jail sentence. Possibly 12 Bengal tigers (*Panthera tigris tigris*) – the type seen by most tourists in India – still exist in Tibet and there are some 18–22 Amur tigers (*Panthera tigris altaica*) in the far north-east,

in the Changbaishan region. This subspecies, which is also found in the Russian Far East (RFE) and possibly in very small numbers in North Korea, is named after the Amur River, which flows through the Russian tiger habitat. Because Amur tigers migrate back and forth across the Sino-Russian border, the tiger's status in the RFE impacts on how it fares in China, too.

^ Flehmen response of a male Amur tiger to pheromones produced by a female: the upper lip is curled back so that her scent can be better detected by the Jacobson's organ, a chemoreceptor on the roof of the mouth.

By the 1940s, when the Amur tiger was dangerously near the brink of extinction, with fewer than 40 individuals left in the wild, Russia had become the first country to grant it full protection by banning hunting. The Cold War also helped, because the forest where the tiger lived was closed to most people. Four decades later, the tiger population had increased to around 500. However, after the collapse of the Soviet Union, poaching and logging increased and populations of deer and other prey species plummeted as they were hunted for food. Nonetheless, thanks to continued conservation and anti-poaching efforts by many organisations, the 2005 Winter Survey of Amur Tigers showed that the population (334–417 adults and 97–112 cubs) had remained stable. But a report released in 2009 by the Siberian Tiger Monitoring Program co-ordinated by the Wildlife Conservation Society managed to count only 56 tigers over an area of 23,000 km² (9,000 sq miles).

It is also now illegal to hunt tigers in China, but they are still poached in Russia for their fur and, if one can be smuggled across the border, the reward is great: its body parts are much used in TCM, despite the fact that this trade is prohibited. The ban, however, does not extend to the sale of alcohol-based health tonics steeped in tiger bone (much in demand during 2010 – the Year of the Tiger). TCM has been responsible for illegal trade across borders in other parts of the tiger's range and was a prime cause of Bengal tiger numbers crashing in India.

Tigers are highly territorial. A male requires a larger area than a female and the Amur, faced with a low density of prey, needs a much larger one than the Bengal, which has plenty of prey to hand. Male territories do not overlap each other, but they may overlap those of one to three females. The typical habitat for the Amur tiger is mixed boreal forest with conifers and deciduous broad-leaved trees, covering mountain slopes and hills. Extremely strong jaws and sharp teeth make tigers superb predators. The Amur's main prey is wild boar and various deer – notably roe and red – but they have been known to kill cattle and horses. Smaller prey is killed by biting the back of the head of the neck, while larger prey is suffocated by grasping the throat. Unlike lions, male tigers allow females and their cubs to feed at a kill before them.

In tropical climates female tigers may breed at any time of year, but the Amur mates during the winter and gives birth in the spring when the weather has warmed up. After a gestation period of 90–105 days, up to six cubs may be born, but a mother usually rears just two or three, suckling them until they are six months old; the male plays no part in their upbringing. When the mother goes off to hunt the cubs are left in a den. She starts to bring them meat when they are eight weeks old; they learn to hunt when they reach a year and stay with their mother until they are two, so in harsh winters she has to find enough prey to feed herself and her cubs.

> As the sun sets, an Amur tiger walks out onto a frozen lake, its breath clearly visible in the very cold air. For a few brief moments, when lit by the last rays of sunlight, the breath looked like a fireball.

ᵛ A tactile tail stroked across the neck is enough to reassure a tiger's mate.

^ Early in the morning, a tiger does what all cats do when they start to become active after a snooze – yawn and have a good stretch.

^ One tiger approaches another and nuzzles up to it, apparently showing some affection.

The Amur tiger is well adapted for surviving severe weather, with a layer of fat on the flanks and belly and a special winter coat with longer and thicker fur. Outsized paws function like snow shoes and thick pads help to fend off the cold. However, when deep snow falls, as it did in the 2009–10 winter, prey has difficulty moving around and avoids badly affected areas, which means the tigers have to work harder to find it. Although it is easy to approach prey silently over soft powdery snow, walking on a frozen crust creates noise, so tigers then either follow in existing animal tracks or walk along iced-over rivers, and may resort to entering villages to devour a dog. With the tigers thin on the ground, attacks on people are now rare, but not unknown.

In July 2009, the WWF opened the first centre in China for studying and protecting the Amur tiger near Hunchun Nature Reserve in Jilin province on the Sino-Russian border. Tiger tracks have been spotted in the region lately and the WWF plans to open two more centres. In the late 1970s, north-west China had around 150 tigers, but by the late 1980s the number had fallen to 35. One of the reasons is that tigers are sometimes trapped in snares set for other animals. Over 5,000 poachers' snares were removed from Hunchun NR in 2002 alone and since then 10,000 have been confiscated.

With so few tigers thought to remain in the mountainous region of north-west China today, the chances of seeing a wild one there are remote. All the tiger images in this chapter were taken at Hengdaohezi Tiger Park in Heilongjiang province. Wildlife photographs can be a powerful tool for arousing public awareness, so it is to be hoped that these and other images will help the plight of this magnificent tiger and make people realise how urgently we need to support all possible ways and means to save it.

Early in the morning we were driven in unheated buses through two sets of double metal gates into a huge enclosure with a thick carpet of snow. Some tigers were already walking around while others were just beginning to wake up, yawning and stretching. With the air temperature around −15 to −20°C (+5 to −4°F) the tigers' breath was visible as a distinct cloud. My own breath froze instantly on the back of the camera. In such weather dressing in layers is essential: with seven layers above and tights, two pairs of long johns, double-layered North Face pants and waterproof trousers below, I felt like a Michelin man, but my body was well insulated all day. Not so my extremities. Three pairs of gloves kept out the cold, but proved quite impractical for depressing small buttons on the camera, so I had to remove one layer; chemical hand warmers inside the gloves helped. Even with foot warmers in my boots, though, my feet never warmed up – probably because they were permanently resting on the bare metal floor of the bus.

> An elaborate ice sculpture in the 2010 Harbin Ice Lantern Festival after the internal lights were switched on at dusk. Huge blocks of very clear ice are cut from the Songhua River to create this ephemeral seasonal spectacle.

>> An Amur tiger races across the snow, sending the frozen crust flying as it stretches out its front legs in readiness to brake.

ᵛ The white spots on the back of the black ears help tigers to see one another in dim light within a forest and are especially useful for cubs trying to keep track of their mother.

This park is one of several tiger farms in north-east China. Here the number of tigers increases annually because it is illegal to sell them, but the food bills spiral upwards. Tigers that die are frozen in the hope that the ban on selling tiger products will be lifted. The farms argue that this would eliminate the need for tigers to be poached, but they overlook the fact that it would be impossible to distinguish captive-bred tiger parts from those of wild animals that had been hunted; so changing the law would almost certainly lead to a speedy demise of this tiger. An encouraging development was a statement made in March 2010 by the World Federation of Chinese Medicine Societies, urging its members not to use tiger bones or any other parts of endangered wildlife species.

With severe winds blowing down from Siberia, sub-zero temperatures are guaranteed for several months in Harbin, the capital of Heilongjiang province, when

144

they may fall as low as −38°C (−36°F). Here, it used to be a local custom for families to make ice lanterns to mark the Chinese New Year. Buckets of water were left outside just long enough for an icy shell to form, then a hole was bored through the shell so that the water drained away, leaving a hollow for a candle. Today, Harbin − known as the Ice City − is the perfect location for an ice festival that has grown from these humble beginnings to become a major winter tourist attraction before and during the New Year celebrations. Over the years it has become more ambitious and more expansive, with companies now sponsoring many exhibits. Elaborate creations − often replicas of famous Chinese architecture, such as the Great Wall or the Forbidden City − are sculpted from large blocks of translucent ice cut from the Songhua River, with coloured lights inserted so that they glow at night. This is a spectacle not to be missed.

< A male South China tiger focuses on the camera lens from within a spacious enclosure at Shanghai Zoo; not all of these critically endangered tigers kept in Chinese zoos are so comfortably housed.

> Framed by leafless trunks, an Amur tiger sits up on a rock – a warmer alternative to snow.

In the southern part of the country, the story of the decline of the South China tiger (*Panthera tigris amoyensis*), one of the smallest of the tiger subspecies, is a tragic one. As recently as the middle of the last century, over 4,000 South China tigers lived in the wild in central and eastern China. Considered 'pests' by the Chinese government, they were ruthlessly hunted after tiger eradication campaigns were introduced. Habitat reduction did not help. Even though this tiger was given special protection in the 1970s, a decade later only 100–200 were thought to exist in the wild. Then, by the turn of the century, the results of a field survey brought even grimmer news. During 2001–2002, researchers working in eight reserves and five provinces, and using two infra-red remote cameras, failed to find any evidence of South China tigers. They also noted that the tiger's prey was very thin on the ground. So, even if a few wild tigers remain in remote forests, the odds are stacked against their being able to breed successfully. Because the South China tiger has not been seen for 20 years it is now regarded as probably functionally extinct in the wild.

However, it survives as a population of captive but highly inbred animals descended from just six wild founders in Chinese zoos and a private South African reserve. Even though the Chinese government is now talking about reintroducing South China tigers to the wild, the remaining captive animals are no longer a pure subspecies, since all have some Indochinese tiger genes. Eyebrows are being raised by some conservationists after four tigers reared in Chinese zoos were released in the private Laohu Valley Reserve in South Africa, where tigers do not occur naturally. This project is the inspiration of Li Quan, who founded Save China's Tigers in 2000. By 2006, three adult tigers had all become proficient hunters and were able to survive on their own. The following year the first South China cub was born in South Africa and now there are five healthy second-generation tigers living there.

When the offspring have learnt to hunt for themselves, a 'rewilding' programme will involve transferring them to vast protected reserves in either Jiangxi or Hunan province in China, where eco-tours are planned. Both Père David's deer (see page 184) and Przewalski's horse (*Equus ferus przewalskii*) became extinct in the wild in China, but have been reintroduced to reserves through captive-breeding programmes. However, these species are both grazers and did not have to learn hunting skills in order to survive. With recent setbacks in the captive-breeding programmes of tigers in Chinese zoos (11 Amur tigers died at Shenyang Forest Wild Animal Zoo during the 2009/10 winter and two of the three cubs born at Suzhou died in 2009), it will be absorbing to see how the innovative yet unorthodox South China 'rewilding' strategy plays out.

Habitat destruction and fragmentation, as well as inbreeding, hunting, poaching and prey depletion, are all contributory factors in the threat to the tiger's survival. It is possible that global climate change will also impact on the future of the Amur subspecies. However, at this eleventh hour huge efforts are being made (and great sums of money expended) to help redress the balance for an animal regarded as the most regal of all the cats. Reserves need to be policed and the sale of all products using tiger parts banned. Education will help to raise awareness; indeed, a tram painted to look like a tiger now plies Hong Kong's streets where this big cat once roamed. At the start of the 2010 Chinese New Year the WWF TX2 Double or Nothing campaign was launched, with the aim of doubling the world's wild tiger population by 2022 – the next Year of the Tiger. Unless major steps are taken to improve the status of wild tigers, their future looks bleak.

CHAPTER 10

WILD HONG KONG

Within half an hour of our boat entering Sha Chau/Lung Kwu Chau Marine Park north-west of Lantau Island, our spotter shouted, 'Port side nine o'clock', alerting us to aim our telephoto lenses on the left side of the bow. A sleek, pale pink mammal broke the sea surface to breathe, then dived and resurfaced repeatedly as we eased our way forward parallel to its course. I could sense the adrenaline rush of this, my first close encounter with a pink dolphin. The population of these dolphins in Hong Kong waters is now estimated to be around only 200, but some 1,400 individuals are thought to live in the nearby Pearl River estuary, so their total numbers are equivalent to those of giant pandas in the wild.

< A pink dolphin surfaces in Sha Chau/Lung Kwu Chau Marine Park, showing its blow hole and narrow pointed beak.

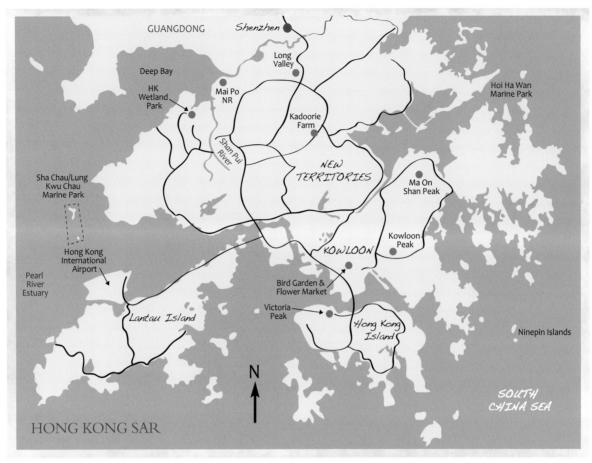

With its tightly packed skyscrapers, Hong Kong's thriving cityscape is hardly a naturalist's paradise. Yet this first view as you approach by air belies the varied natural areas beyond. There are beautiful beaches, gentle forest trails, challenging hill walks, numerous islands; the diverse wildlife includes globally rare birds and corals – not to mention the dolphins. The green side of Hong Kong is now being promoted with dolphin-watching tours, organised field trips and the opening of a National Geopark. The northern-hemisphere winter is a good time for wildlife-viewing; for one thing, the weather is a pleasant 10–18°C (50–64°F) and for another the typhoon season (May to September) has passed. Situated at 22° N, Hong Kong lies just within the tropics and has a similar monsoon climate to that of southern China.

With time to spare in any overseas city I always make a beeline for the botanical gardens. Here, the wildlife – especially birds – are habituated to people and so are more approachable than in a wilderness location.

In tropical countries, conspicuous red flowers such as hibiscus attract bird pollinators; nectar and pollen supplies in smaller flowers lure butterflies, bees and moths. Studying native plants in botanical gardens is an excellent way to become familiar with their distinctive features, aiding identification in the field, where there are no convenient labels.

On Hong Kong Island the Hong Kong Zoological and Botanical Gardens (HKZBG) are perched on the mid-levels of the northern slope of Victoria Peak. Here can be found many Hong Kong orchid trees (*Bauhinia blakeana*); although not remotely related to orchids, they have exquisite deep pink orchid-like flowers set amongst bilobed leaves. This striking native is a popular urban street tree in the tropics and since 1997 has become the floral emblem of the City of Hong Kong, replacing the Queen's head on all coins. It also appears on the flag as a stylised white flower within a red background.

Camellias originate from eastern Asia – particularly China and Japan – and many are popular in gardens,

> Crapnell's camellia fruit is the size of a cannonball – the largest fruit of any camellia.

ᵛ The pink flowers of the Hong Kong orchid tree. The leaves of this plant resemble a butterfly with open wings, reminiscent of childhood days when we folded paper in half to cut out symmetrical shapes.

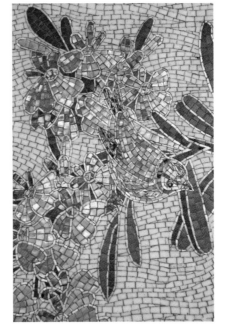

^When Crapnell's camellia flowers open in December they attract day-flying moths.

< One of several bird mosaics featured in the Bird Market on Yuen Po Street in Mong Kok, where Hong Kong's songbird owners bring their caged pets out for an airing.

in both the East and the West. In the HKZBG I spotted a shrub bearing outsized single white flowers with a central cluster of yellow stamens, superficially like a fried egg sunny side up. My initial instinct was that it had to be a camellia, but huge brown fruit introduced a niggling doubt. Nevertheless, the label revealed it was Crapnell's camellia (*Camellia crapnelliana*), which I later learnt produces the largest of all camellia fruits and grows in woodlands on two Hong Kong peaks, Lam San Ting (also known as Mount Parker) and Ma On Shan.

Within the forest surrounding Gilwell Camp Site on Kowloon Peak, the peace was shattered by a gaggle of mountain bikers – with well-padded elbows and knees – bouncing down the stone steps, oblivious to the inhabitants of the stream they raced across. I, too, would never have known a threatened amphibian was breeding there if I had not chatted to post-graduate students after I lectured at The University of Hong Kong. They were eager to show me some of the local specialities, including the Hong Kong newt (*Paramesotriton hongkongensis*). Once thought to be endemic to Hong Kong, this is now known to exist also along the coastal part of Guandong province. From above, it blends in with a brown stream bed, so it would have to be photographed in an aquarium. However, because it is protected in Hong Kong, it could not be collected. The solution was to transfer a few newts to an aquarium beside the stream, photograph them and then return them to their habitat so that their water temperature remained constant.

^ The upper surface of the Hong Kong newt is uniformly brown – a good camouflage when resting on a brown stream bottom.

This meant a trip to Tung Choi Street in Mong Kok to buy an aquarium – an experience in itself. It was packed with aquarists' shops, some with every conceivable variety of highly bred goldfish – butterfly tails and bubble eyes, to name but two. I spotted some diminutive alligator snapping turtles (*Macrochelys temminckii*), looking positively primeval with long tails. I pondered the fate of these reptiles bought by customers who had no inkling they would grow into monsters weighing on average up to 80 kg (175 lb).

Vivian Fu, who was researching the Hong Kong newts, had arranged for a friend to drive us up Kowloon Peak. We must have looked a curious pair – me with my camera gear and aquarium; Vivian carrying a net and wearing flip flops for wading. On reaching the stream, Vivian waded in searching for newts, while I collected stones to create a naturalistic setting within the aquarium. My hosts were too polite to make any comments, but as soon as we introduced some newts to the tank, they dived for cover beneath the stones. Then it dawned on me that they must be nocturnal! I had no option but to remove the rocks so that they had nowhere to hide.

Hong Kong newts are uniformly brown above with deep orange spots on their bellies. Just as a human fingerprint is unique, so the belly-spot pattern is unique to each newt. Researchers photograph newt undersides and use a software program capable of recognising the spot pattern so that individuals can be identified and their migration movements plotted. In autumn the Hong Kong newt migrates over land to pools in clear hillside streams with large rocks and aquatic vegetation, where they breed during the winter, so this was a perfect time to locate them.

< A female Hong Kong newt swims up to reveal her belly pattern, which is unique to each individual. Females lay their eggs one at a time, wrapping each one in waterside vegetation.

> The belly pattern of a male Hong Kong newt showing a random arrangement of spots. During the breeding season the male displays by beating his tail, which develops a white or bluish stripe that is just visible in dim light.

^ A great cormorant (*Phalacrocorax carbo*) colony in Mai Po Reserve.

Mai Po Marshes Nature Reserve, on the north-west coast of the New Territories (NT), is famous as a bird reserve and it is a crucial part of the internationally important Deep Bay wetland. As well as the birds, it is worth visiting for a diverse flora, many insects – notably dragonflies in summer – and the fauna of the mangrove swamp. Managed by WWF Hong Kong, it forms part of the region's biggest wetland habitat, between north-west Hong Kong and Shenzhen in mainland China, and requires a permit to visit. The Agriculture, Fisheries and Conservation Department (AFCD) controls access to the

site. In 2010 there was a revival of the annual Hong Kong 'Big Bird Race', first organised by WWF Hong Kong in 1985 as a fundraiser, whereby several teams compete for the most birds seen.

In autumn and winter, when thousands of migratory birds converge here, Mai Po becomes a birdwatcher's paradise. Two special winter visitors are Saunders's gull (*Larus saundersi*), a small gull with a short, black bill and a black hood on breeding birds; and one quarter of the world population of black-faced spoonbills (*Platalea minor*). Situated midway along the East Asian–Australasian

154

^ A group of black-faced spoonbills gather to feed at Mai Po.

> The long-legged black-faced spoonbill can wade into deep water to feed.

Flyway (EAAF), Mai Po and Inner Deep Bay provide a vital stop-over for birds to refuel on the intertidal mudflats before they continue on to Australia and New Zealand. Here the mangrove swamps, reedbeds, freshwater ponds, mudflats and man-made *gei wai* (tidal shrimp ponds) are all part of the Deep Bay wetland.

Across the water on the north side of Deep Bay there is now a forest of skyscrapers in Shenzhen city. As recently as the late 1970s Shenzhen was a small fishing village, but foreign investment has made it one of the fastest-growing cities in the world and southern China's major financial centre. Deep Bay has suffered increasing pollution, probably because of this intense urbanisation.

Alien plant species are causing another negative effect on Mai Po. The northern shore of Deep Bay was reclaimed for building and, to help preserve the land, exotic mangrove species such as the rapidly growing *Sonneratia apetala*, which originates in Bangladesh, were planted. Their seedlings float across Deep Bay to Mai Po, where the reserve staff constantly have to remove this vigorous alien by hand to prevent it choking out the smaller and slower-growing native species.

The multifarious islands – both large and small – that lie within the Hong Kong SAR provide a varied array of maritime habitats, ranging from rocky shores to sandy beaches and from mangrove swamps to volcanic islands. For me, the mangrove swamps are especially fascinating. Seven of the eight true Hong Kong mangrove species occur at Mai Po and each has different types of roots that help to support the plants when exposed at low tide. As the tide recedes, fiddler crabs begin to emerge from their burrows in the soft mud to forage on detritus. Each male has one outsized pincer, which he uses to signal to other males that this is his territory, as well as to attract females. He uses his smaller pincer to delicately pick up detritus from the surface of the mud.

> Little egrets (*Egretta garzetta*), here wading as they feed in Kam Tin River, can also be seen at Mai Po, together with great egrets (*Egretta alba*).

< A photo sequence showing how a male fiddler crab plugs his burrow hole in a mangrove swamp.

ᵛ The single large pincer and stalked eyes become visible as a male fiddler crab emerges from his burrow in a mangrove swamp at low tide.

Good places to see fiddler crabs at close range are on either side of the floating boardwalk, accessed via a gate controlled by the Hong Kong police and necessitating a Closed Area Permit. At low tide, crabs and mudskippers – curious fish that frequent tropical estuaries and mangrove swamps, emerging at low tide to feed on the detritus and micro algae – move over the exposed mud, whereas high tide pushes the waders close to the bird-watching hides at the end of the boardwalk overlooking Deep Bay.

Because I was there at low tide for the crabs, the birds were a long way off, so on hearing my camera shutter clicking repeatedly an enthusiastic birder, anxious he might have missed something, asked what I was taking. When I replied, 'Mudskippers', he retorted, 'You don't take fish from a bird hide!'

The sheltered bay that comprises Hoi Ha Wan Marine Park lies in the north of Sai Kung Country Park and is known for its diversity of marine life, notably corals and

< Like fiddler crabs, mudskippers (*Boleophthalmus pectinirostris*) emerge at low tide to feed on detritus, inching forward by rowing on their pectoral fins. Their tracks remain visible in the mud until the tide turns.

ᵛ *Kandelia obovata* is a mangrove that flowers all year round. Its fruits gradually produce long droppers that aid dispersion by floating in the water before taking root.

reef fish. When the WWF Marine Life Centre was constructed here in 2003, great care was taken to limit environmental damage and to protect the shallow-water coral community. The centre was built on an area of coral-free seabed and, to minimise pollution, rubbish and noise, most of the prefabricated superstructure was built off-site and transported by barge. Sadly, it was too rough for me to take a ride in Hong Kong's first glass-bottomed boat, which allows visitors to gain an insight into some of the underwater life.

Not far from Mai Po, as a bird flies, is Long Valley, which has the largest remaining area of wetland agriculture in Hong Kong.

Thanks to traditional farming of wet fields, it attracts numerous birds and is one

∧ A milky mangrove (*Exoecaria agallocha*) showing copious roots exposed at low tide in Hoi Ha Wan Marine Park.

< Rock oysters (*Saccostrea cucullata*) attached to the stem of a mangrove (*Aegiceras corniculatum*).

of Hong Kong's prime birding sites. It was threatened when the Kowloon–Canton Railway wanted to build a viaduct through the middle of the area, but the HK Birdwatching Society led a campaign opposing the project, as a result of which a tunnel was built beneath Long Valley. The speciality of the area is the elusive greater painted snipe (*Rostratula benghalensis*); using binoculars we saw two birds well camouflaged in amongst the spinach. In 2009, a year after my visit, a pair bred successfully. Black-winged stilts (*Himantopus himantopus*) were resting amongst some pak choi, typically standing on one of their ridiculously long pink legs. This habit is a way of keeping one leg warm beneath the feathers when the water or ground is cold; once warmed up the legs can be swapped over.

159

So to the legendary pink dolphins – my prime target
for this trip. They are the pink form of the Chinese white
dolphin (*Sousa chinensis*), known outside Hong Kong and
mainland China as the Indo-Pacific humpback dolphin.
They frequent coastal waters in the western Pacific and
Indian Oceans, extending from South Africa in the west
to southern China and north Australia in the east. Their
colour is unique among maritime dolphins, but one
freshwater species, the Amazon River dolphin (*Inia
geoffrensis*), is also pink.

Pink dolphins have been known to exist in Hong
Kong waters for more than three centuries. In 1657, the
British explorer Peter Mundy spotted them as he sailed
along the Pearl River, which enters the sea along Hong
Kong's west coast. But not until the late 1980s did they
begin to hit the headlines when their favourite areas were
discovered off northern Lantau, adjacent to the island of
Chek Lap Kok, then earmarked as the site of Hong Kong's
new airport. Several years later, when work started on the
airport, this provided the impetus to research the impact
the construction – including land reclamation – might
have on the dolphins. By 2005, the AFCD census for
Chinese white dolphins frequenting Hong Kong waters
showed that they fluctuated with the seasons. The spring
low of fewer than 100 animals doubles by the autumn.

But even though the Sha Chau/Lung Kwu Chau Marine
Park was set up in open waters on the western side of
Hong Kong in 1996 specifically to protect the dolphins,
enforcing the regulations is by no means easy. While we
were dolphin-watching, a trawler crisscrossed part of the
area, its telltale muddy wake showing that it had been
illegally trawling the bottom.

Not all the dolphins are pink; newborn calves have
more skin pigments and so appear grey. As they age, the
pigments are lost or become more dispersed, making
the juveniles dappled grey with some pink areas. Older
dolphins lose all the pigments and appear white – or pink,
due to blood vessels lying close to the skin surface.

Unlike bottle-nosed dolphins, Chinese whites move
around in small pods; once weaned, the calves leave their
mothers. This dolphin has an unusual diving posture, first
lifting its slender beak out of the water as it arches its back,
then pausing before dipping below the surface or flipping
its tail to dive. When speed is essential, it will leap
repeatedly out of the water, since air offers less resistance
to its body than water. Dolphins also spy-hop by emerging
vertically from the water to see what is going on.

Researchers are able to distinguish dolphins by the
shape and position of the dorsal fin – unique for each
indivdual. Using photographs, they build up an ID bank

to track the passage of individual dolphins. Animals with a slash on the dorsal fin or other parts of the body are the lucky ones that have survived close encounters with boat propellors.

A group of keen bird photographers took me to the Sha Pui River to see winter waders. This river made the news in November 2003, when local villagers discovered a 1.5 m (5 ft) long crocodile. It was a juvenile female saltwater crocodile (*Crocodylus porosus*), a native of South-East Asia, New Guinea and northern Australia – but not of Hong Kong. For seven months, Pui Pui, as she became known, evaded capture by some of the world's most experienced crocodile hunters, before being caught and eventually transferred to Hong Kong Wetland Park. Her enclosure here is positively Ritz-like, with infra-red heaters hidden beneath rocks to provide warmth on cold nights,

<< An adult pink dolphin swims in Hong Kong waters with its grey calf behind. As the animal matures, the skin pigments fade and the grey areas shrink to reveal more pink.

^ Three pink dolphins surface showing the variable profile of their dorsal fins. These marine mammals are threatened by the changes brought about by Hong Kong's rapid economic development.

v An immature estuarine crocodile (not Pui Pui) swims underwater, its limbs pressed against its body to make a streamlined profile.

a water-filtration system to maintain pool-water quality, and even hidden scales to record her weight. It is thought that this alien species ended up in a Hong Kong river when the illegal pet became too large to handle.

> Organisms that live on the rocky shore have to be able to withstand pounding by crashing waves, as here on Stanley Prison beach in the southern district of Hong Kong.

ᵛ A colourful mosaic of aquamarine sponge, pink coralline alga, barnacles and a topshell exposed at low tide on the rocky shore of Stanley Prison beach.

Eager to explore life on rocky shores, I could have no better guide than Professor Gray A. Williams, Honorary Director of the Swire Institute of Marine Science at The University of Hong Kong. He told me winter was the best season for intertidal life, because this is when the larger leaf-like seaweeds regrow after being killed off during the scorching summer temperatures; these can make the shores appear barren, although oysters and mussels are still present. The invertebrate types are similar to those found in Britain – colourful sponges encrust rocky overhangs, limpets and marine snails graze the rocks – although the species are quite different. Mobile animals such as limpets and both herbivorous and carnivorous types of marine snail inhabit sheltered rocky shores, while mussels and barnacles attach themselves to exposed rocky shores and feed by filtering particles from the turbulent sea.

Quite by chance, I was able to join a boat trip to the Ninepin (Kwo Chau) group of islands. Some 140 million

< Fruit on a female screwpine tree on Bluff Island. After fruits fall to the ground they split up and float out to sea where they are dispersed by ocean currents; the seeds within remain viable for many months.

ˇ Hexagonal columns on North Ninepin Island in Hong Kong Geopark.

years ago, volcanic ash and lava were disgorged by a series of large eruptions; when the hot ash slowly cooled it formed an extensive area of volcanic hexagonal columns on the North Ninepin Islands. Landing here is never easy and the sea was just too rough the day we visited, but we had fine views of the columns as we circumnavigated the island. We were able to land on Bluff Island, where a strip of screwpine (*Pandanus tectorius*) 'forest' backs onto the foreshore. These evergreen trees have saw-like margins to the leaves and the lower stem is supported by prop roots. A year later the Ninepin Island Group, together with seven other sites, became incorporated into the Geopark.

Here is a taster of what awaits keen naturalists in Hong Kong, where 40 per cent of the terrestrial territory is protected – one of the largest quotas in eastern Asia.

CHAPTER 11

PRECIPITOUS PEAKS

Huangshan or Yellow Mountain has long been famous for its peculiarly shaped rocks, distorted rock-clinging pine trees, views down onto a sea of changeable clouds, and hot springs. Whatever pathway you take, many peaks appear, peppered with conifers misshapen by the weight of snow and ice. Only when you visit Huangshan can you appreciate that the wizened conifers growing out of barren rock faces, depicted in Chinese ink-brush paintings, really do exist in nature.

< Peaks fringed with Huangshan pines silhouetted at sunrise within the Behai or North Sea area. In 1990, Huangshan was designated both a cultural World Heritage Site (for the temples and monasteries) and a natural WHS (for the scenery and the rare plants and animals). Then in 2004 UNESCO declared it a World Geopark.

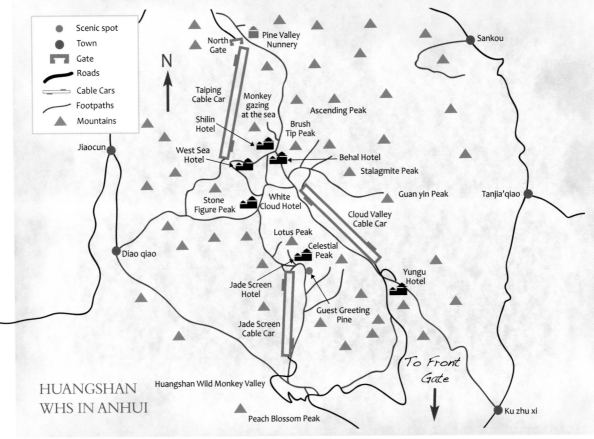

Legend:
- Scenic spot
- Town
- Gate
- Roads
- Cable Cars
- Footpaths
- Mountains

N

North Gate
Pine Valley Nunnery
Taiping Cable Car
Monkey gazing at the sea
Ascending Peak
Shilin Hotel
Brush Tip Peak
Jiaocun
West Sea Hotel
Behal Hotel
Stalagmite Peak
Stone Figure Peak
White Cloud Hotel
Guan yin Peak
Tanjia'qiao
Cloud Valley Cable Car
Lotus Peak
Diao qiao
Celestial Peak
Yungu Hotel
Jade Screen Hotel
Guest Greeting Pine
Jade Screen Cable Car
To Front Gate
Sankou
Ku zhu xi

HUANGSHAN WHS IN ANHUI

Huangshan Wild Monkey Valley

Peach Blossom Peak

South of the Yangtze River, in the south of Anhui province, lies Huangshan – a mountain like no other. Xu Xiake, a noted traveller of the Ming Dynasty (1368–1644), described it as the loveliest of all Chinese mountains and there is an old saying, 'Once you have seen Huangshan, there is no need to see any other mountain.' Here there are many granite peaks ranging from 600–1,864 m (1,970–6,114 ft), with 77 of them over 1,000 m (3,280 ft). The oldest sedimentary and metamorphic rocks were formed over 570 million years ago by uplifting from the ancient Yangtze Sea. Later on, granitic rocks formed when magma erupted through fissures. The rocks were shaped by erosion; glaciation created U-shaped valleys and left boulders perched on rocks.

During the Qin Dynasty (221–206 BC), the mountain was known as Yishan, but was renamed Huangshan from the legend that it was from here that the Yellow Emperor ascended to heaven and became immortal. When Buddhism took the place of Taoism at the end of the Ming Dynasty, Buddhist monasteries were built on the slopes. Artists, poets and literary scholars have also revered the mountain for centuries: in the mid-16th century, painters working in the *shanshui* (mountain and water) style came to admire and paint the scenic views.

As is typical of mountains, the vegetation has distinct zones. Below 1,100 m (3,600 ft) is moist mixed forest, with evergreen ring-cupped oak (*Cyclobalanopsis glauca*) and Masson pines (*Pinus massoniana*) dominant up to 800 m; up to the treeline at 1,800 m (5,900 ft) Huangshan oak (*Quercus stewardii*) and Chinese beech (*Fagus engleriana*) flourish in deciduous forest. Trees then give way to alpine grassland. Between 800 and 1,800 m (2,600–5,900 ft) the Huangshan pine (*Pinus hwangshanensis*) occurs. It is regarded as an example of vigour because it can grow from apparently inhospitable rock crevices – the more distorted the tree the more it is prized. Century-old trees are so revered that they have been given their own names.

^ Snow-covered locks in the Behai Sea area. 'Locking your love' is an ancient Chinese custom, whereby a couple place a padlock on a chain: providing it remains in place, their love will last forever.

> Worn smooth by weathering, a light-coloured granite peak with Huangshan pines is isolated by rising cloud. Despite its name, the pine is not confined to this mountain, where it can grow with little soil at higher levels than most broad-leaved trees.

< The distinctive fan-shaped leaf of the maidenhair tree (*Ginkgo biloba*) turns a glorious golden colour in the autumn. It is one of several endangered plants that grow on Huangshan.

Outside the central core zone of the reserve is the buffer zone, where 45 per cent of the area remains as natural forest. Here, the moist climate favours the growth of tea and the mountain is famous for Mao Feng – one of China's finest green teas.

The Huangshan mammals include the Asian black bear, clouded leopard, wild boar, Asiatic wild dog or dhole (*Cuon alpinus*) and rhesus and Tibetan macaques. At the middle and lower elevations, mixed evergreen and deciduous forests are home to several troops of Tibetan macaques, which sleep here in caves or rocky crevices. But one of the most bizarre mammals has to be the Chinese pangolin (*Manis pentadactyla*): with horny scales instead of hairs covering the body, it can roll itself into a ball as a protection against predators. Rarely seen because it is solitary and nocturnal, it has long claws for digging and a long sticky tongue; it can devour a staggering 70 million ants and termites a year.

< Just below the Behai Hotel, the pine tree on top of the Brush Tip or Gifted Writing Brush Peak resembles a flower that blooms throughout the seasons. One of many poems written to praise the beauty of this rock formation says, 'A nature-made gifted brush paints all the lovely scenes.'

> Snow on peaks and Huangshan pines.

∨ Snow-covered pine needles coated with a thick hoar frost.

By 2008, Huangshan attracted 2.24 million visitors, including many artists, photographers and poets. On my first visit, in 1988, the only way to reach the famed scenic spots was by climbing hundreds of steps, taking either the Eastern steps route (easier) or the Western steps (rugged, but more picturesque), so I requested a porter to help carry my gear. When a slip of a girl – even shorter than me – turned up, I was taken aback, but she did the job brilliantly. Now that there are three cable cars it is possible to go up and down one part of the mountain in a single day, but you still need several days to trek the serpentine paths and you won't see a sunrise unless you stay on the mountain.

In 2009, I set aside five days in December. Long before reaching Huangshan, I checked the weather forecast daily and was delighted to see that 'torrential' snow with plummeting temperatures was forecast towards the end of that period, so I bought a couple of pairs of cheap crampons in Huangshan city. This time I dispensed with a guide on the mountain, since I knew the Shilin Hotel and the many paths leading out from it; but I did hire a porter to carry my basic gear – photo pack, tripod, laptop and cold-weather clothing – from the top of the cable car to the hotel.

Some of the outlooks are narrow, with limited prime spaces. It is therefore essential to rise early, leaving when it is still dark to claim a spot before sunrise (preferably wearing a head torch for climbing up the stepped paths), because serious photographers who stagger up the mountain with their panoramic or full-frame-view cameras know precisely where to go for the best shots. Then there are the Chinese tourists, who often prefer to stand with their back to the view and have their picture taken in front of it. Being short, I usually managed to squeeze into a front spot with taller guys shooting over me.

169

^ A natural still-life study: frost decorates rhododendron leaves overnight after a snowfall. Rhododendrons are one of many flowering shrubs that grace Huangshan.

> Granite peaks rise island-like above a sea of clouds that ebbs and flows around them.

On the fifth day it began snowing at breakfast time and continued all day, so I decided to extend my stay. I had my favourite viewpoint virtually to myself – almost all the tourists and keen photographers who had been there during the previous fine weather evaporated. It is hard work photographing in heavy snow, but with the camera on a tripod protected with its own waterproof cover plus an umbrella held overhead, it is doable. Even so, miniature snowdrifts soon accumulated inside the lens hood and had to be repeatedly scooped out. Everywhere I walked, staff were busy chipping away the down-trodden snow that had been frozen into icy sheets – near the Behai Hotel I noticed that even some of the chefs were out, wearing their high white hats (maybe all they had?). It was just as well I had invested in four crampons, for the rubber straps broke on two of them and I ended up with one intact pair.

The greatest attraction of any single lofty snow-capped peak is to view it from below against a blue sky. With

Huangshan, it is to look down onto the sea of clouds that forms after rain or snow falls, when the atmosphere is very humid. The clouds begin to rise, spreading out like a sea below, separating one peak from another until the tops resemble islands. Wind also shifts the clouds, billowing them in and out of gullies and ravines. Even though the heaviest rainfall is produced by summer thunderstorms from May to August, the sea of clouds is rarely seen then; it appears most often during the winter.

As the temperature drops, rhododendron leaves roll in on themselves and hang down vertically; then as the weather warms up they open out as they gradually rise again. But the most amazing phenomenon associated with sub-zero winter weather on Huangshan is the exaggerated hoar frost or rime that develops on trees and shrubs when the humid air is constantly blown through them. The undersides of pine trees can look completely white, with a copious frost-laden layer covering the needles. The weight of snow and ice on the pines prunes the tops and breaks branches, so that flattened umbrella shapes are not uncommon. Topography and weather combine to create the ever-changing features that make Huangshan so appealing.

South-west of Huangshan lies another multi-peaked mountain – the Wulingyuan Peak Forest, which I had arranged to visit a month later to compare the two scenic areas in the off-peak season.

171

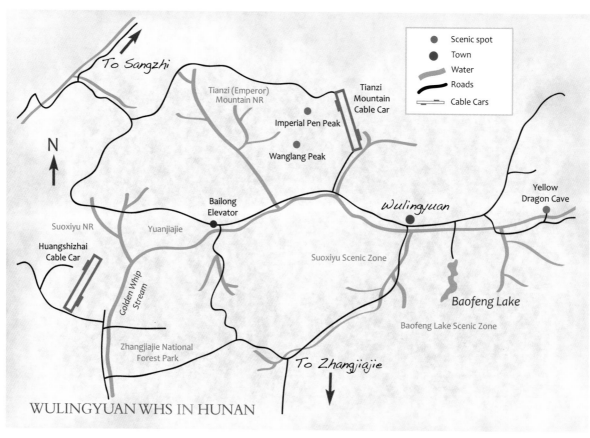

WULINGYUAN WHS IN HUNAN

The unique landform of Wulingyuan Peak Forest (rebranded as Zhangjiajie after Dayong city was renamed Zhangjiajie city in 1994) lies 390 km (242 miles) to the west of Changsha, the capital of Hunan province. Access is easy from Zhangjiajie city, a mere 40 minutes' drive away. Unlike Huangshan, Wulingyuan's fame does not stretch back for thousands of years: rugged and inaccessible, it remained unknown to all but local inhabitants until the latter part of the twentieth century. In the 1970s, the Chinese master painter Mr Wu Guanzhong found it by chance and was fascinated by its beautiful scenery, which he described as '…a bright pearl, unknown in the depth of the mountains'. After a painting he made of the area was published, photographers began to flock there.

Here, over 3,000 slender – mostly sandstone – peaks and columns rise up from deep secluded ravines. The long straight faces were formed when flat-topped mesas became fragmented into peaks and columns as fractures developed down vertical joints.

The Wulingyuan Scenic Area consists of three parts: Tianzi (Emperor) Mountain Nature Reserve to the north, Zhangjiajie National Forest Park to the south-west and Suoxiyu Nature Reserve to the east. There are three ways to ascend to the scenic spots – via two cable cars and one elevator. Eco-friendly buses transport you from the entrance to the base station of all three, so it is important to check you board the correct bus. Here, my guide proved invaluable, but having now seen the lie of the land, armed with a map I could cope on my own another time. The various scenic areas are extensive, but free buses ply back and forth between them, so it is not nearly such hard work as climbing up and down the stepped pathways on Huangshan. The Tianzi cable car goes up to Tianzi Mountain where Imperial Pen Peak can be seen, but with the Huangshizhai cable car under repair, Suoxiyu NR was inaccessible. The Bailong elevator travels up the side of a high cliff, making the lower third of the journey through rock and the rest outside it, whizzing up 335 m (1,100 ft) in just under two minutes.

^ A silhouette of the pine-covered Apeman Peak in the Yuanjiajie area.

> Wulingyuan pines (*Pinus massoniana wulingensis*) on a sandstone column in Wulingyuan (Zhangjiajie) Peak Forest grow from seemingly inhospitable soil-free rock.

∨ The fern-like foliage of dawn redwood (*Metasequoia glyptostroboides*) as it turns colour in autumn. This deciduous conifer occurs on Wulingyuan and is now classed as critically endangered in the wild.

^ The Imperial Pen Peak cluster on Tianzi Mountain is the signature formation of Wulingyuan; its geology is so significant that the area was designated as Zhangjiajie Sandstone Peak Forest World Geopark in 2001.

As well as the sandstone peaks, one third of the Wulingyuan reserve is limestone, with notable karst features including 40 caves along the banks of the Suoxi River and to the south of Tianzi Mountain. The 11 km (7 mile) long Huanglong or Yellow Dragon Cave is one of the ten largest in China. Many streams drain into Suoxi River, which runs through the centre of the site, and a side branch of the river has been dammed to create Baofeng Lake, used as a water source, for flood control, to extend the habitat of the endangered giant salamander (*Andrias davidianus*) and as a boating amenity for tourists.

A delightful and relatively gentle walk takes you beside the pristine waters of the Jinbianxi (Golden Whip Stream) through the base of a canyon bordered by steep cliffs and into a forest where many trees anchor themselves with roots growing around large boulders. Where the soil has been eroded from beneath, the roots of trees growing beside the stream resemble giant spiders about to pounce on their prey. The walk crisscrosses the stream where the giant salamander still resides; in recent years some captive-bred animals have been introduced here (see page 176).

Wulingyuan has a humid mountainous subtropical climate with an average annual temperature of 16°C (60°F), a January mean of 4.8°C (40°F) and a July mean of 27.3°C (81°F). April and October are the most congenial months to visit, with autumn having the bonus of vibrant colours from maples and other trees. Snow may fall in December and January but, as the area is further south than Huangshan and not as high, snowfall tends to be less frequent. The subtropical monsoon climate produces much rain, particularly in June and early July, when the stone pathways can be slippery and the views from the summit may be blotted out by thick fog. At other times of year, a sea of clouds forms a few hours after snow or rain falls, helping to define and separate peak clusters from a rocky backdrop.

While I was on Wulingyuan, a local television company arrived to film a piece about some of the columns being the inspiration for the floating Hallelujah

^ Silhouetted peaks fade into the distance in Wulingyuan Peak Forest – a World Heritage Site since 1992.

↓ Camellia flowers and leaves littering a rock beside Jinbianxi (Golden Whip Stream) early in January were tell-tale signs that rhesus macaques had been feeding in an overhanging tree.

Mountains in the Hollywood blockbuster *Avatar*. Shortly afterwards, the spot was renamed Avatar Hallelujah Mountain as an advertising gimmick to boost tourism.

As with Huangshan, arranging a winter visit to coincide with snow or frost is something of a gamble. Waiting to fly into Huangshan Tunxi airport until a frigid weather forecast looks set is risky, since the airport closes during foggy weather – as I discovered after I descended from the mountain on my last day and had to make a 14-hour train journey back to Shanghai to connect with my flight home. A guide who was on Wulingyuan in mid-February sent me stunning shots of dramatic rime coating the vegetation, which appears on only a few days in the year. The descriptions 'spectacular' and 'awesome' apply to both of these primeval-looking landscapes, to which I shall return in spring and autumn to see a richer palette of nature's colours.

Back FROM THE BRINK

Much has been written about China's recent rapid economic expansion having a negative effect on the environment. While it is true that pollution and habitat loss – particularly in the eastern part of the country – have been detrimental to wildlife in general, many people are now actively working to redress the balance. This section focuses on five species that live in wetlands – habitats that are greatly affected by drainage and pollution. In each case, efforts are being made to protect them within special reserves, and captive-breeding programmes are on-going. Education must also play an essential part in raising public awareness of the fact that endangered species need all the help they can get.

CHINESE GIANT SALAMANDER

COMMON NAMES
Chinese giant salamander
Dani
Baby fish

SCIENTIFIC NAME
Andrias davidianus

IUCN RED DATA LIST STATUS

Past distribution
Found in clean mountain streams in tributaries of the middle reaches of the Yangtze, Yellow and Pearl Rivers from 200–1500 m (650–4,900 ft).

Current status
The wild population has plummeted in the latter part of the 20th century from over-harvesting to provide luxury food for banquets

Each female lays strings of 500 large yolky eggs that the male fertilises externally. After 50–60 days the larvae hatch with a yolk sac that nourishes them for a month until they are able to feed on aquatic insect larvae.

Longevity
There are stories of giant salamanders weighing over 100 kg (220 lb). One captive animal in Hunan, aged 90 in 2009, then weighed 65 kg (143 lb).

Threats
- Habitat degradation and destruction
- Dam construction
- Fragmentation of wild populations
- Illegal collection for luxury food trade and as ingredients for TCM
- Lack of suitable breeding burrows or caves
- Females are sensitive to disturbance during the breeding season.

Description
The world's largest amphibian, it once reached up to 2 m (6 ft 6 in) in length; now usually only half as long. The large flattened head has tiny eyes lacking eyelids, and small nostrils just above the upper lip. A skin fold running down each side of the body increases the area for oxygen absorption.

Basic needs
Unpolluted streams or clear running lake water with a pH close to neutral, a winter temperature above 8°C (46°F) and a summer temperature that does not exceed 25°C (77°F).

Food
Adults feed on crustaceans and fish, but will also eat other amphibians and freshwater molluscs. Prey is sensed by vibrations in the water and sucked into the huge mouth. Both jaws have many small teeth able to grip even larger prey effectively. Essentially a nocturnal species, giant salamanders become active during the day when breeding.

Breeding
This occurs when they reach 5–6 years and weigh 2–3 kg (4–6 lb). In August/September mature males seek out a breeding burrow or denning cave. They make calls like a baby crying (hence the name baby fish) and females respond with a similar call. The male guards his den against other males but allows females to come and go.

> This fossil of a Chinese giant salamander shows the huge jaws armed with many tiny teeth.

FUTURE PROSPECTS

There are now 17 giant salamander reserves in China, including the Zhangjiajie Chinese Giant Salamander NNR. To ensure that wild populations are maintained and ultimately increased, adequate funding, sympathetic management, habitat protection, poaching control and a conservation action plan are required. The largest artificial-breeding and protection base was recently completed in Sanzhaolun Forest Park in Jiangxi province, where salamanders are bred for scientific research, the TCM industry and public aquaria. Elsewhere, breeding farms have been licensed to produce them for food and beauty products; individual households are also licensed for small-scale breeding. Salamanders are gradually being reintroduced into the wild – 1,000 were released into streams in Jiangxi in May 2005.

CHINESE STURGEON

COMMON NAMES
Chinese sturgeon
Zhong Hua Xun

SCIENTIFIC NAME
Acipenser sinensis

IUCN RED DATA LIST STATUS
Endangered (EN)

⌐ Painting of a Chinese sturgeon in the Yangtze River at the ICS at Yichang.

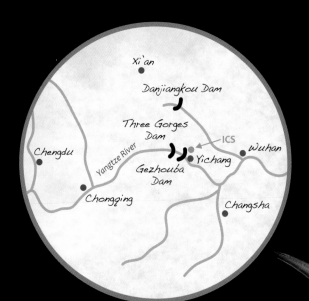

Past distribution
In coastal waters of the East China Sea and Yellow Sea, from where it migrated 3,500 km (2,000 miles) to the upper reaches of the Yangtze River (the Jinsha) to spawn. In 1981 the route was blocked when the Gezhouba Dam was completed.

Current status
Enters the coastal waters of the Chinese continental shelf to feed and grow before returning to the Yangtze to breed. Two decades ago there were some 2,000 adult sturgeon in the river, now probably fewer than 500. Since 1984 the Institute of Chinese Sturgeon (ICS) in Yichang has used a synthetic compound to induce females to produce eggs; over five million captive-bred sturgeon have been released into the Yangtze. Sturgeon damaged by boat propellers that have been restored to health at the ICS now have a chip bearing an alpha-numeric code inserted under the skin before release.

Description

Sturgeon have an underslung mouth and an asymmetrical tail with a larger upper lobe. The Chinese sturgeon can grow up to 5 m (16 ft) in length – the size of a bus – and weigh 200–500 kg (440–1100 lb).

Basic needs

Like salmon, migrates from the sea into fresh water to breed. Takes 11–14 years to mature in the coastal waters of the East China Sea and Yellow Sea before returning to fresh water.

Food

Bottom feeder, using barbels that hang down from the lower jaw to feel for worms, shrimps, molluscs and small fish.

Breeding

Migrates up the Yangtze River to breed. Used to leave the delta in June/July and spawn in the upper Yangtze in November. After the migration journey was curtailed to 3–7 km (1.8–4 miles) downstream from Gezhouba Dam, a special conservation area was set up here, but the total spawning grounds now cover less than 30 km (19 miles) compared with more than 600 km (375 miles) previously. Each female lays up to one million (average 0.6 million) large black eggs, but only about 1 per cent hatch. At ICS, with the water temperature between 18°C and 20°C (64–68°F), the larvae hatch after 4–5 days, each with a large yolk sac that nourishes it for the first two weeks of life.

Longevity

Estimated at 80 years for females, which make only three migrations to spawn in a lifetime; the males, which mature earlier, live for 50 years.

Threats

- Dams are a barrier to migrating fish
- Piers of major bridges slow down the river and disrupt the movement of migratory fish
- Illegal fishing
- Boat propellers
- Noise pollution (can cause disorientation)
- Pollution from industrial run-off below the Gezhouba Dam is causing sturgeon to change their sex ratio. This used to be one to one, but since 1995 in some years there can be as many as ten females to one male.
- Triphenyltin (TPT), used in anti-fouling paints on ships' hulls, has been found to cause deformities in 30 per cent of sturgeon fry.
- An estimated 90 per cent of eggs and young fry is eaten by bronze gudgeon (*Coreius heterodon*) on the present spawning grounds.

ᵛ Underside of a Chinese sturgeon, showing barbels for feeling along the bottom.

FUTURE PROSPECTS

Although this ancient species that once lived alongside the dinosaurs is strictly protected by the Chinese government, the number of adult sturgeon found in the Yangtze has dropped dramatically. Now that access to its traditional spawning grounds is blocked and its sojourn in the river is fraught with hazards, the survival of this megafish depends, to a large extent, on the captive-breeding programme at the ICS.

CHINESE ALLIGATOR

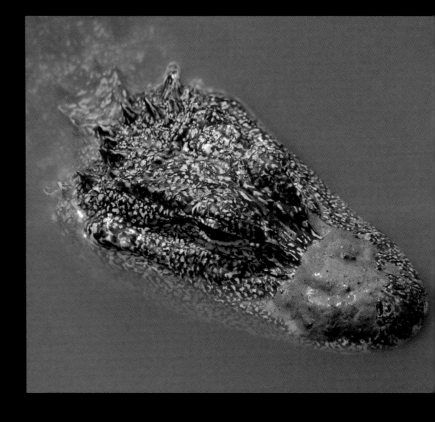

COMMON NAMES
Chinese alligator
Yangtze alligator
Tu long or muddy dragon

SCIENTIFIC NAME
Alligator sinensis

IUCN RED DATA LIST STATUS
Critically endangered (CR), under 130 in the wild,
making it the most endangered of the world's
23 crocodilian species

Past distribution
In provinces covering the lower Yangtze, Anhui,
Jiangsu and Zhejiang. Habitat loss has been
the prime cause of plummeting populations,
exacerbated by slaughter of the alligators
themselves and persistent use of pesticides.

Current status
Found only around the lower Yangtze in the
Anhui Chinese Alligator NNR where, in 2003,
three captive-bred individuals were released in
an 8-ha (20-acre) artificial lake used to irrigate
rice paddies. Between 2006 and 2009 27 more
were released in Gaojingmiao forest farm (an
area of 1,400 ha/3,460 acres) in Anhui province.
In 2007, six captive-bred Chinese alligators
(including three from Bronx Zoo, New York,
to increase the genetic diversity) were released in
Chongming Island at the Yangtze River mouth,
and 15 active offspring were seen in 2008.

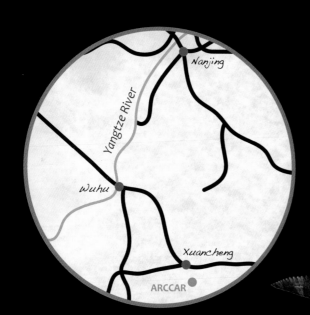

Description
One of the smaller crocodilians, reaching 2 m (6 ft 6 in) in length with a slightly upturned snout. The scales on the belly are ossified, making the skin worthless on the international market.

Basic needs
Lakes, swamps, slow-moving streams and rivers or agricultural areas up to 100 m (300 ft) above sea level, where it lives a largely solitary and nocturnal life. Spends half the year hibernating in elaborate burrow systems with multiple chambers where the temperature rarely falls below 10°C (50°F). Begins to emerge from its den to bask in April.

Food
Between May and October hunts chiefly at night for freshwater snails, mussels, crayfish and fish, using specially adapted teeth to crush mollusc shells. However, like any crocodilian, it is an opportunistic feeder, grasping anything which comes within reach of its jaws, including frogs, snakes, birds, rats and even wild rabbits.

Breeding
Females are able to breed at six to seven years old. A nest mound is made from decaying vegetation and nesting takes place in July, with a clutch of 10–50 eggs being laid. The baby alligators take 70 days to incubate within the nest, with the sex of the young determined by the temperature at which they are incubated; males are mostly produced at above 33°C (91°F), although they are also produced at 30–32°C (86–90°F). If the temperature is lower than that, the young will be female. Juveniles have a distinctive disruptive coloration – black with bright yellow cross-banding.

Longevity
Can live up to 50–60 years.

Young captive-bred Chinese alligators at the ARCCAR surface to breathe.

Threats
- Habitat destruction, notably conversion of marshland into agricultural land
- Fragmentation of remaining wild populations
- Flooding, notably in 1957
- Conflict with humans: burrows can cause flooding in fields and alligators will take farmed ducks
- Illegal killing from fear, with alligator parts sold in markets for TCM, even though the reptile is protected.

FUTURE PROSPECTS

The Anhui Research Centre of Chinese Alligator Reproduction (ARCCAR) opened in 1979 and began to breed alligators in 1982. The captive-breeding programme has been successful in terms of numbers, with 10,000 alligators now on site, but genetic investigation has revealed an extremely low genetic diversity. Therefore, maintaining captive populations both in China and overseas is essential. Alligators introduced to the wild on Chongming Island (six in 2007) and in Anhui (six in 2008) have had their movements followed with radio tracking devices. Within the next decade, the aim is to create suitable new habitats before reintroducing captive-bred alligators to the wild to boost the wild population to 400 individuals.

CRESTED IBIS

COMMON NAMES
Crested ibis or Asian crested ibis
Toki (Japan)

SCIENTIFIC NAME
Nipponia nippon

IUCN RED DATA LIST STATUS
Endangered (EN)

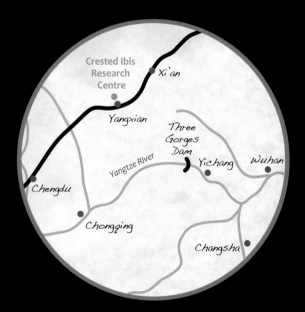

Past distribution
Used to breed in the Russian Far East, Japan and China, and was a non-breeding visitor to North Korea, South Korea and Taiwan.

Current status
Now found in the wild only in a small area in Yangxian county, Shaanxi province, within China's central wetlands.

Description
White bird with red face and legs and a black, downwardly curved bill. The crest gives the bird its common name and the plume feathers, sought after as hat ornaments, resulted in many birds being hunted. In breeding plumage, the crest, head, neck and back appear grey.

Basic needs
Shallow wetland areas to feed and tall trees (usually pine or oak) to roost and for nesting.

Food
Uses the long curved bill to extract freshwater fish (especially loach *Misgurnus anguillicaudatus*), shrimps, crabs, frogs and freshwater snails from beneath stones or among aquatic plants. Also feeds on beetles and other invertebrates on adjacent grasslands.

^ Wild crested ibis gather in a tree to roost at dusk in Yangxian.

Breeding

After a courtship period in March birds mate and a nest is built close to the trunk of a pine or oak tree. The female lays up to four eggs, but the pair usually raises only 1–2 chicks.

Longevity

The last two captive birds on Sado Island in Japan were believed to be 26 years old when they died.

History

From the 1960s to 1980s populations rapidly decreased. The last ibis departed the Russian Far East in 1963 and Korea in 1979. In 1981 the remaining five in Japan were transferred from Sado Island to the Sado Crested Ibis Conservation Center (SCICC), where they died out by 2003. For three years the ornithologist Liu Yinzeng surveyed areas in China where the bird used to live and in May 1981 he found the last seven (four adults and three young) wild crested ibis in Yangxian county on the southern slopes of Qinling Mountains in Shaanxi province. Intensive management has led to the Chinese population increasing to about 600 birds in the wild, 100 at the Breeding Centre in Yangxian and others at Beijing Zoo by 2009. Ten birds were given to Japan in September 2008 and a pair to South Korea the same year. Before supplementary feeding of loach began in 1981, the breeding success averaged only 38 per cent; from 1982 to 2004 it averaged 64 per cent.

Threats

- Low genetic diversity
- Accidental poisoning along the Han Sui River where it regularly feeds
- Winter starvation
- Asian flu outbreak

FUTURE PROSPECTS

Great strides have been made since 1981. Captive breeding at the Shaanxi National Ibis Breeding Centre and reintroduction to the wild have increased the population sufficiently for some birds to be dispatched to Beijing Zoo. One wild bird is added each year to enhance the zoo's gene pool. Logging, hunting with firearms and the use of agrochemicals are now prohibited (farmers are compensated for this) in Yangxian county. But with dry wheat fields replacing many wet rice paddies, fewer winter feeding sites exist, so some ibis starved to death until loach were added to flooded paddies in winter. Ibis nest-sites are safe-guarded during the breeding season by wardens and farmers. Since a crested ibis was spotted on the southern Yangtze in April 2008 – for the first time in 50 years – the future looks hopeful for this spectacular bird.

PÈRE DAVID'S DEER

COMMON NAMES
Père David's deer
Milu or *sibuxiang*

SCIENTIFIC NAME
Elaphurus davidianus

IUCN RED DATA LIST STATUS
Extinct in the wild (EW)

> Père David's deer stags stand up to box in winter as the second sets of antlers start to appear.

Past distribution

Endemic to swampy areas in north-east and east-central China. Hunting and wetland drainage resulted in virtually all wild deer disappearing by the late 19th century. Since the Yuan Dynasty (1205–1368), the Nanyuang Royal Hunting Park on the outskirts of Peking (now Beijing) was stocked with animals for the Emperor and from 1616 a herd of milu was kept there. When Père David spied the deer over the wall in 1864, he realised they were unknown in the West. Fortunately, some were sent to Europe before the Nanyuang deer were almost wiped out in 1895 by a catastrophic flood which breached the wall, allowing many of them to escape. The rest were killed for food during the 1900 Boxer Rebellion when troops invaded the Imperial Park. Initially the deer sent to Europe (known by then as Père David's deer) were kept on the Woburn Abbey estate, but on the outbreak of the Second World War they were dispersed to various European zoos.

Current status

Reintroduced to China from Europe in the 1980s as captive managed populations. The Beijing Milu Park was created on the old site of the Royal Hunting Park. In 1986, 39 deer were released into Jiangsu Dafeng Milu Reserve beside the Yellow Sea. By the end of 2009, the population had risen to 1,502 in one of the largest wetland reserves in Asia. The deer have also been introduced to Tianezhou Milu NR beside the Yangtze River and to Yuanyang Yellow River NR.

Description

The Chinese name *sibuxiang* ('unlikes') relates to features which resemble bits of other animals – the hoofs of a cow, head of a horse, antlers of a deer and tail of a donkey. Stags grow two sets of antlers in a single year: the larger summer ones are dropped in November after the rutting season; a smaller second set appears in January and is shed a few weeks later. The growth form

^ Herd of Père David's deer in January at Dafeng Milu NNR.

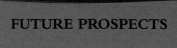

of the antlers is unique among deer, with the
points extending backwards. These deer are good
swimmers and use their large splayed hooves
to break ice that forms in winter when bitter
winds blow in from the sea.

Basic needs
Wetlands with open water and marshy land
providing favourite food plants.

Food
Grasses, especially swamp foxtail grass (*Pennisetum
alopecuroides*), and aquatic plants in summer.

Breeding
Becomes mature in the
second year. During the
rutting season in June a
male starves, spending
all his time and energy

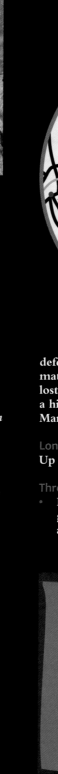

defending his harem from other stags. After
mating, he feeds avidly in order to regain his
lost weight. After a nine-month gestation period,
a hind gives birth to usually one calf between
March and May.

Longevity
Up to 18 years.

Threats
* Limited suitable natural habitat (limited
genetic diversity does not appear to be
a problem).

FUTURE PROSPECTS

Chinese populations are steadily increasing
at a rate of 17 per cent and more each year
without apparent effects of inbreeding. With
four separate reserves, the risk of disease
spreading is much reduced. Late in 2009, 192
deer were living in the wild outside Jiangsu
Dafeng Milu NNR and if free-ranging
populations become established the status
will need to be revised.

TRAVELLERS' TIPS

Things to know before travelling to China

- Avoid the Chinese New Year, when virtually the whole of China is on the move and hotels charge premium rates. The dates (from late January to mid-February) vary each year, but they can be found on the Internet. The Golden Week (first week in October) is also very busy.
- Get a tourist visa before leaving your country of origin (see Visas below).
- Currency in the People's Republic of China is Renminbi (RMB), with banknotes ranging from 1–100 yuan. Renminbi is the official name (like Sterling) and yuan (CNY) is the base unit (like the pound). Hong Kong has its own currency, the Hong Kong dollar (HK$). Take either currency or US dollar traveller's cheques to change in China.
- Planes may be cancelled at short notice. This happens more often in remote places or in the off-peak season, but can occur at any time of year due to bad weather, rescheduling of planes or if not enough seats have been sold.
- The time quoted to get from A to B can be optimistic, as most drivers don't use maps and only a few have sat navs. This is not a problem in their local area or on expressways, which have clear signs. But when travelling away from their home territory, drivers often get lost, have to stop to ask the way and may even retrace their tracks.
- Heavy rain, especially in mountain regions, may cause landslides or undercutting of the road, involving a detour or a change of itinerary.
- Don't drink tap water. Either boil it or use bottled water.
- The time is GMT + 8 hours. Despite the vast size of the country, Beijing time is standard throughout China.
- The official language in mainland China is Mandarin Chinese, but there are many dialects. In Hong Kong, English and Chinese (most people speak Cantonese) are the official languages. Learning a few useful common words and phrases in Mandarin will be appreciated by Chinese people – especially in remote areas.

Joining a tour

For first-time travellers this is the easiest option, but even so it pays to research as much as possible to ensure that the trip caters for your needs.

Cultural tours to China are well established, whereas eco-tours are quite novel. A few, with a guide from the country of origin, are available from Western wildlife tour companies (see below). Each year, Chinese operators are running more eco-tours of varying length, so it is possible to combine two or three short tours on a single trip. Be sure to check each tour's aims and objectives, what proportion of the day will be spent travelling and what is left for exploring at each stop; also whether they supply an English-speaking guide.

Western travel agents who run eco-tours to China

Greentours
Botanical trips *http://www.greentours.co.uk*

Naturetrek
Botanical trips to Yunnan and Sichuan *http://www.naturetrek.co.uk*

Sunbird Tours with Wings (USA)
Birdwatching tours *http://www.sunbirdtours.co.uk*
http://wingsbirds.com

Wildlife Worldwide
Tailor-made trips to see pandas, golden monkeys and crested ibis
http://www.wildlifeworldwide.com

^ On a windswept high-mountain pass at 4,000 m (13,100 ft) in Sichuan, lichens and an attractive alpine (*Sibbaldia* sp.) hug the ground.

Agents in China who run eco-tours

China Bird Tours
Formerly Golden Bridge Travel, this was the first travel service inside mainland China to specialise in birding tours. Now run by Jia Min (Kate Jia), who speaks English and has organised many tailor-made tours for me all over China.
http://www.birdschina.com

Expeditionschina Company Ltd
Michael Deng is a fixer and English-speaking guide for photographers and wildlife tours. *http://www.expeditionschina.com*

Guilin Photo Tours
The only Chinese tour operator specialising in photo tours of the Guilin area. Contact: Pan Shijun, who has run several tailor-made tours for me.
http://www.guilinphototours.com

Haiwei Trails
Based in Zhongdian in Yunnan, HWT was the first 'adventure' travel outfit to focus exclusively on south-west China (Yunna, Sichuan, Gansu) and Tibet.
http://www.haiweitrails.com

Yunnan Overseas Travel Corporation
Manager Michelle Yang (Yang Wenying) has organised several tailor-made tours for this book. *http://www.toptrip.cc*

The following are well established, but not experienced first-hand:

Eco-tour China
Offers a range of tours across China and Tibet. *http://www.ecotourchina.com*

Pepper Mountains
Innovative tours that explore the nature and culture of western China.
http://www.peppermountains.com

^ The resplendent plumage of this male mandarin duck (*Aix galericulata*) shows why it is a popular species in ornamental wildfowl collections.

Planning your own trip

Alternatively, you can plan your own trip with good maps and much research. I rely on several travel agents in China who are used to arranging naturalist tours.

Detailed bird and plant lists produced either by individuals or by tour companies (often in their tour reports) can be found on the Internet. I research the best time to go – when birds are nesting or certain plants are in flower, for example – and sketch out a rough itinerary. At this stage, I don't always know how long it will take to fly or drive from A to B and how well the flights connect, although this information, too, is on the Internet.

You need to decide whether you want a driver, car and guide throughout the trip or just to get from one place to the other, so that the Chinese operator can send you a quote. If it is too expensive, request ways in which the cost can be reduced – taking the train will be cheaper than flying, but usually a lot slower. The best sites are rarely at the end of a railway line or bus route, so a local bus or taxi may be needed for the last leg.

Check if meals and entrance fees are included in the quote. I prefer to exclude both. I cannot eat any wheat- or milk-based products, so I have to be selective and usually end up ordering a dish of stir-fry vegetables, which are cheap. For anyone over 65, it is worth showing your passport to get a reduced fee to scenic areas and national parks, although some places don't offer it until you reach 70. To save money, use a shuttle bus to get to and from a hotel to the airport. If one is not available, a taxi is cheaper than a car and a driver. Always get a price for the taxi before you set off.

The Maglev train that connects Shanghai's Pudong airport with the outskirts of the city is the first commercial high-speed Maglev line in the world. It takes just 7 minutes 20 seconds to cover 30 km (18 miles). You will still need to take a taxi or the Metro to reach a hotel.

Visas

To enter China you need a tourist visa, which will not be issued more than 90 days before departure. Single-entry visas are valid for three months from date of issue, double-entry for six months. These are obtained via the appropriate Chinese Embassy or their visa office. Holders of British or US passports do not need a visa to visit Hong Kong.

To enter Tibet you need: a valid passport, a valid Chinese visa, a Tibet Tourism Bureau (TTB) permit to enter Tibet and an Alien Travel Permit (PSB) if you are planning to travel to the 'unopened areas'. If you book a tour outside China, the agent will arrange a Tibet permit; you cannot get one in China without booking a tour there. Requirements can change at short notice.

Embassy of the People's Republic of China in the UK

49–51 Portland Place, London W1B 1JL, UK. Tel: (020) 7299 4049 *www.chinese-embassy.org.uk*, from where the visa form can be downloaded: it must be printed out on both sides of a single page. To visit the visa office you need an appointment, which can be made via the website.

Embassy of the People's Republic of China in the USA

2300 Connecticut Avenue, NW, Washington, DC 20008, USA Tel: (202) 328 2500 *www.china-embassy.org*

Getting to China

By air

When I first began to visit China in the mid-1980s I had no option but to fly to Beijing or Hong Kong. Now there are international airports all over China and the list is expanding each year.

By train

Take the Trans-Siberian Railway to Moscow and then the Trans-Mongolian or Trans-Manchurian line to Beijing.

By sea

The following is a selection of popular routes:
UK: Southampton to Hong Kong and Shanghai
USA: Seattle and Los Angeles to Shanghai; Seattle to Hong Kong
Canada: Vancouver to Shanghai; Vancouver to Hong Kong
Japan: Osaka to Shanghai and Tianjin
South Korea: Incheon to Shanghai, Tianjin, Qingdao, Weihai and Dalian

Transport within China

By air

Internal flights are the most cost-effective and speediest way of getting around: they are cheaper if you book in advance and travel in off-peak seasons.

By rail

The fare varies according to the type of seat: hard seat, soft seat, hard sleeper and soft sleeper. Children under 1 m (3 ft) tall travel free and those under 1.3 m (4 ft) pay just 25 per cent of the adult fare.

High-speed trains are gradually being introduced between the main cities.

The Qinghai to Tibet railway – the highest rail route in the world, climbing to 5,072 m (16,640 ft) – was opened to passengers in 2006. The trip to Lhasa from Xining takes 24 hours and is an experience in itself. Before you travel you have to sign a declaration that you are fit to do so; oxygen is supplied in all carriages. From Beijing the train to Lhasa takes almost 48 hours and from Shanghai 51 hours. See *http://www.chinatibettrain.com/index.html*

By road

New expressways are being built each year, speeding up journeys to remote locations. Hiring a car is not practical for short visits, since you need a three-month residency permit and an examination before you can get a local licence. Cars with a driver can, however, be hired on a daily or weekly basis. Few drivers speak English, so help will be needed to establish routes and the cost. Long-distance buses tend to be crowded and take forever.

Where to stay
Hotels

Tourist hotels are very variable in the services they provide. In an attempt to clarify what is on offer, various rating systems have been introduced.

Essentially, as elsewhere, the more stars the better the service and facilities you can expect. The criteria used to decide the category include the architecture, quality of service, facilities available, maintenance, sanitation and hygiene, security for guests and, not least, guest satisfaction.

5 stars – the finest hotels with luxury rooms, excellent service and multiple restaurants including a coffee shop. Many belong to a worldwide chain of superior hotels.

4 stars – a good restaurant, lounge and room service

3 stars – comfortable with staff willing to help, but not all speak English

2 stars – clean, basic accommodation

1 star – basic accommodation for the budget traveller

Western brand-name 5- and 4-star hotels will have staff at the front desk who speak English and there will be a breakfast buffet with Western food. There will be Internet connections in the rooms, business centres, money-changing facilities, conference facilities and a range of restaurants including Western, Chinese and possibly also Japanese, Italian or French.

The 5- and 4-star Chinese hotels will have many of the above facilities, but the range of food may be limited: for instance there may be only a Chinese-style breakfast.

In mid-scale hotels the restaurants tend to be Chinese, targeted at both Chinese and other Asian business travellers and also the increasing number of Chinese tourists with their new-found surplus cash. Staff at the front desk may speak little or no English, but Chinese tourists who speak English are often very helpful. The Hanting Inns and Hotels group focuses on the mid-scale market, with all branches located in main sightseeing spots: *http://ir.htinns.com*

In small cities often only 2- or 3-star Chinese hotels are available; then the best option is a Chinese economy hotel chain such as:

Jinjiang Inns *http://www.jinjianginns.com/en*

Home Inns *http://english.homeinns.com*

Super 8 *http://www.super8.com.cn/en*

The rooms may be small, but they are clean, with Internet access and hot water. In older hotels at the bottom of the scale, maintenance of the electrics and plumbing tends to be non-existent and the cleanliness of the rooms poor.

Homestay in the countryside

This is a reasonable option if you don't want to cart camping gear throughout your trip, although it is wise to carry your own sleeping bag in cooler months. I have stayed in local village houses in Yunnan, some of which now have lightweight duvets instead of heavy blankets. The food is often better here than in hotels catering for Chinese tourists. The owners are unlikely to speak English,

^ Framed by bamboos, an ephemeral waterfall cascades through a fern carpet after an overnight storm in the South Sichuan Bamboo Sea.

but they will be very willing to please and you can always mimic eating and write down a meal time, to which they will react by either nodding or shaking their head. The only downside can be the loo: usually this involves a trek across a courtyard – not ideal in the middle of a wet night. Wash basins are invariably outside, but the lights attract an extensive insect fauna at night, which my husband enjoyed photographing! The shower, if present, is enclosed in an outhouse or a room attached to the house.

Camping

This is a very economic way to travel, especially if you buy food in markets. As yet, the Chinese do not recognise camping as we know it in the West with specifically designated campsites. However, I have camped in several places, including a walled orchard within a monastery on a plant-hunting trip to Yunnan. We were woken at first light by the monks chanting, but that was preferable to yaks munching outside the tent throughout the night with their neck bells clattering as they walked over alpine pasture. The problem may be to find a secluded place off the beaten track.

Youth hostels

Advice from someone who has used them is that they may be dirty and damp, but are a great place to meet other backpackers and to share travel experiences.

Ordering food in China

If I don't have an English-speaking guide, I resort to one of the following options:
- In cities and resorts, menus are supplied with colour pictures of dishes.
- Some high-volume tourist restaurants have plastic models of dishes.
- Small street eateries usually allow me to wander through the kitchen and point to what I want.
- If all else fails I have the names of some basic dishes such as egg and tomato stir-fry written in Chinese in my notebook.

Cities and tourist resorts

Hotels in the main resorts – especially those that cater for foreign tours – are well kitted out with plugs for the basin and bath (though these don't always fit properly), loo paper, soap, face cloth, kettle and increasingly an Internet connection in the room (often but not always free). Instant coffee and tea bags are now readily available from supermarkets or 7-Eleven shops.

General China checklist

- **Photocopies of passport, Chinese visa and airline tickets**
- **Mobile phone**
  - buy a Chinese one with a pay-as-you-go package (pay in cash so your card cannot be debited after you leave China).
  - if you have a Triband or Quad band international GSM cell phone, buy a prepaid SIM card in China to put in it.
  - before leaving home, check with your mobile phone operator that your phone is unlocked for global roaming.
- **Mains adapter** for charging leads for laptop, mobile and camera batteries. There are three types of socket in China – three square-pin 13 amp in the newest hotels in big cities, otherwise two-pin round pin or two-pin flat pin. *http://users.telenet.be/worldstandards/electricity.htm* is a useful site with an illustrated guide to which plugs to use in which countries.
- **Solar-powered recharger:** there are several models available, for recharging mobile phone and digital SLR batteries in the field or when a power cut occurs.
- **Plugs** for basin/bath
- **Loo paper:** this was like gold dust in the mid-1980s. Now restaurants supply tissues which are worth bagging for use in public loos in towns – although I would rather find a bush than use some of these.
- **Ear plugs** – to block out sounds from street traffic or a karaoke bar!
- **Pen knife** for peeling fruit (place in checked baggage)
- **Travelling alarm clock**
- **Wet wipes**, especially for use on dusty roads
- **Alcohol gel** for cleaning hands when there is no water or towels
- **First-aid pack**
- **Mask or bandit scarf** that pulls up over the face as protection against dust or aerial pollution
- **Soap** and **face cloth**
- **Mosi-guard**, which deters biting insects for hours
- **GPS** for checking altitude
- **Wind-up torch:** use anywhere, at any time
- **Head torch:** useful for keeping both hands free
- **Shower caps** from hotels: a handy first-stage protection for cameras in rain or snow while you put an umbrella up
- **Head umbrella:** keeps both hands free. You can buy one in China for around 10RMB (£1 or US$1.50).
- **Field notebook:** mine lives in my photo vest and is my bible in three ways:
  - For speedy reference to my day-to-day itinerary with flight numbers, departure and arrival times, plus guides' names with phone numbers in case of delay
  - To show rangers or wardens photocopied images of animals or flowers I want to find (I paste these in before I leave home)
  - To record names of locations, plants and animals I photograph (with local names, TCM uses, etc.), habitat, weather and elevation as well as smells and sounds, which cannot be captured in a photo.

SUB-ZERO TEMPERATURE CHECKLIST

- **Waterproof beanie hat** plus **ear muffs** or **hat with ear flaps**
- **Padded jacket** (long padded coats worn by Chinese women are cheap in China)
- **Balaclava** or **neck warmer** to pull up over chin, mouth and nose
- **Silk underwear:** unglamorous, basic long johns and long-sleeved tops are cheap in China
- **Thick, padded trousers**
- **Ski goggles** or **sunglasses**
- **Undergloves** to wear inside a waterproof and windproof pair (chunky ski gloves are hopeless for depressing small buttons on cameras)
- **Chemical hand warmers** and **foot warmers**
- **Arctic winter boots** with thick soles, designed to keep feet warm for hours on frozen ground
- **Spiky pavement crampons** that slip on over boots as ice grips: essential when climbing myriad ice-covered steps on mountains such as Huangshan. The rubber straps on cheap crampons I bought in China for 30 RMB (£3 or US$4.50) broke on the first day.
- **Hot-water bottle** for hotels in areas without central heating, where lobby entrances are freezing in winter. Most rooms have heaters and some supply electric blankets, but a HWB is good insurance. In China small HWBs come with a power lead for reheating directly from the mains.

TROPICS & SUBTROPICS CHECKLIST

- **Battery-operated fan** or **safari pith helmet**
- **Large-brimmed hat** or **Tilley hat** (rainproof, will float and has a secret pocket in the crown to stow important items)
- **Sunscreen**
- **Water bottle** that fits in a holster or into a pouch in a belt
- **Platypus hydration system** – provides a hands-free drink when on the go; if you use an insulating sleeve, water will keep cooler for longer
- **Water purification tablets**
- **Absorbent towel** to wear around the neck
- **Drip-dry shirts** and **trousers**
- **Compass** – lighter and cheaper than a GPS
- **Waterproof stuff sacks** to keep clothing, cameras, food etc. dry when wading through rivers
- **Leech socks** for tropical rainforests in the wet season.

^ Purple beautyberry (*Callicarpa* sp.) fruits persist on branches after leaf fall, providing valuable late winter food for wild birds.

BIBLIOGRAPHY

This bibliography is an eclectic collection of books that are either in my own library or that I have found useful. Many on the general list, such as identification guides covering all China, apply to every chapter. The unequal length of the references for each chapter reflects what is currently available either in English or with an English summary or lists of scientific names. Hong Kong has a lengthy list because English is one of the two official languages and many more books are published in English there. I have included books in Chinese with lists of scientific names because I found these valuable in providing the first link of a – sometimes lengthy – nature detective trail for gleaning scraps of information about a plant or animal. Armed with the scientific name of a plant, I could search the eFlora of China website (see below) and find its elevation, geographical range, habitat type, flowering and fruiting times. Scientific names also help to unearth common English names – especially if the plant is cultivated – as well as providing leads to scientific papers on the latest research.

General

Angel, Heather, *Green China*, Stacey International, 2008 (a review of major habitat types)

Chapman, Phil, et al, *Wild China: natural wonders of the world's most enigmatic land*, BBC Books, 2008 (relates to the BBC series *Wild China*; DVD also available)

Feng Kuomei, *Rare and Precious Wild Flowers of China*, University of British Columbia Press, 1997

Gascoigne, Bamber, *The Dynasties of China*, Robinson, 2003 (rev edn)

Gong Xi & Zhang Qitai, *Wild Ornamental Fruit Plants from Yunnan China*, Chinese Corporation for Promotion of Humanities, 2003 (Chinese & English bilingual)

Gong Xun et al, *The Rare and Endangered Plants in Yunnan China*, Chinese Corporation for Promotion of Humanities, 2006 (Chinese with scientific names)

Jach, M.A., & L. Ji, *Water Beetles of China*, Vienna Natural History Museum (Entomology), Vols 1–3 1995, 1998, 2003

Keys, John D., *Chinese Herbs,* Charles E. Tuttle, 1976

Laidler, Liz & Keith Laidler, *China's Threatened Wildlife*, Blandford, 1996

Li Shuanke (editor-in-chief) *Scenic Splendor of China*, Chinese National Geography; English edition New Star Press, 2006)

Liu Ying (trans. Zhou Xiaozheng), *Natural Wonders in China*, China Intercontinental Press, 2007

MacKinnon, John, *Wild China (Wild Places of the World)*, New Holland Publishers 1999 (2nd edn)

MacKinnon, John, & Karen Phillipps, *A Field Guide to the Birds of China*, Oxford University Press, 2000

Mansfield, Stephen, *China Yunnan Province*, Bradt Travel Guide, 2007 (2nd edn)

Murray, Geoffrey, & Ian G. Cook, *The Greening of China*, China Intercontinental Press, 2004

Sivin, Nathan, et al, *The Contemporary Atlas of China*, Weidenfeld & Nicolson, 1988

Smith, Andrew T., & Yan Xie (eds), *A Guide to the Mammals of China*, Princeton University Press, 2008

Songqiao, Zhao, *Physical Geography of China*, Wiley, 1986

Songqiao, Zhao, *Geography of China*, Wiley, 1994

Temple, Robert, K.G., *China Land of Discovery and Invention*, Patrick Stephens, 1986

Walters, Martin & Heather Angel (photographs), *Chinese Wildlife*, Bradt Travel Guides, 2008

Wang Hesheng, *Floristic Geography of North China*, Wanhai Books, 1997 (in Chinese with an index of the seed plants in North China)

Winchester, Simon, *The River at the Centre of the World*, Penguin Books, 1998

Winchester, Simon, *The Man Who Loved China*, Harper, 2008

Xu Zhihui (editor-in-chief), *Natural Museum: Nature Reserves in Yunnan*, China Forestry Publishing House & Yunnan Unversity Press, 1999

Yang Chunyan (ed), *Rare Wild Animals*, Foreign Languages Press, 2002

Yi-Fu Tuan, *A Historical Geography of China*, Transaction Publishers, 2008

Zhao Ji et al, *The Natural History of China*, Harper Collins, 1990

Useful websites

http://www.arkive.org the ultimate multimedia guide to the world's endangered species includes text, images, video clips and sounds.

http://www.conifers.org the Gymnosperm Database

http://www.efloras.org/index.aspx lists floras by country

http://www.iucnredlist.org the IUCN Red List of Threatened Species™

http://www.nationalparkofchina.com/cnnp.html National Parks of China

http://gis.wwfus.org/wildfinder part of the WWF USA site. Wildfinder is a map-driven searchable database of more than 26,000 species worldwide.

http://www.worldwildlife.org/home.html information about projects WWF is currently working on and about endangered species.

Maps

Gizi map series China
1. South China
2. Central China
3. Northeast China
4. Northwest China
5. Tibet

Useful map websites:

http://www.themapshop.co.uk

http://www.stanfords.co.uk

http://www.maps.com

Trekking in Tangjiahe

A Report of the Comprehensive Survey on Tangjiahe Nature Reserve in Sichuan, China, China Intercontinental Press, 2005 (Chinese with scientific names)

The Bamboo Sea

Fu Maoyi, *Sustainable Management and Utilization of Sympodial Bamboos*, Beijing: Huayu Nature Book Trade, 2007

Meredith, Ted Jordan, *Timber Press Pocket Guide to Bamboos*, Timber Press, 2009

http://www.bamboosea.net/english/travel/index.asp

Life-giving water

Chan, S., et al (eds), *Directory of Important Bird Areas in China (Mainland)*, BirdLife International, 2009 (Chinese with English summary)

Gosney, Dave, *Birding in China* (DVD), Gostours, 2007

Griffiths, Mark, *The Lotus Quest: in search of the sacred flower*, Chatto & Windus, 2009

Xiangwen, Zou, *Flowering Lotus of China*, Jindun Publishing, 1997 (Chinese & English bilingual)

China's national treasure

Angel, Heather, *Giant Pandas*, Evans Mitchell Books, 2006

Angel, Heather, *Panda*, David & Charles, 2008

Harkness, Ruth, *The Lady and the Panda*, Nicholson & Watson, 1938

Schaller, George B., *The Last Panda*, University of Chicago Press, 1993

Schaller, George B., Hu Jinchu, Pan Wenshi & Zhu Jing, *The Giant Pandas of Wolong*, University of Chicago Press, 1985

http://www.panda.org

http://pin.primate.wisc.edu/factsheets/entry/golden_snub-nosed_monkey

Hot springs and rainforests

Stotz, Douglas F., et al (eds) *China: Yunnan, Southern Gaoligongshan*, The Field Museum – Rapid Biological Inventories, Chicago Field Museum of Natural History, 2003 and online

http://www.fieldmuseum.org/research _collections/ecp/ecp_sites/rapidinvento ries/index.html)

Wang Huasha, *Mt. Gaoligong: a land of well-preserved primeval ecosystems*, Yunnan Fine Art Publishing House, 2004 (Chinese & English)

Xiaohua, Jin, & Xiaodong, Zhao (eds), *Native Orchids from Gaoligongshan Mountains, China*, Chinese Corporation for Promotion of Humanities, 2009 (Chinese with scientific names)

http://www.redpandanetwork.org/red panda/links.php

Karst, caves, cormorants and carp

Cao Lei, *Guilin*, Foreign Languages Press (1998)

Runhua Yang, *Soul of Landscape Photography: a photo traveller's guide to Guilin*, Lingnan Meishu Chubanshe, 2007 (English, Chinese, French & German)

Yuan Daoxian, *Karst of China*, Geological Publishing House, 1991

Following the plant hunters

Alpine Garden Society Expedition to China 1994, A. G. S. Bulletin, vol.64, No.2, 1996, pp122–266

Alpine Garden Society Expedition to China 2002, The Alpine Gardener, A. G. S. Bulletin, vol.70, No.3, 2002, pp254–375

Cowan J. M. (ed), *The Journeys and Plant Introductions of George Forrest*, Oxford University Press for the RHS, 1952

Cox, E. H. M., *Plant Hunting in China*, Oxford University Press, 1945

Cox, Peter, & Peter Hutchison, *Seeds of Adventure: In Search of Plants*, Garden Art Press, 2008

Feng Guomei, *Rare and Precious Wild Flowers of China*, Volume 1. (Series: Rare and Precious Wild Flowers of China 1), China Forestry Publishing House, 1996

Flanagan, Mark & Tony Kirkham, *Wilson's China a Century on*, Kew Publishing, 2009

Haw, Stephen G., *The Lilies of China*, Timber Press & Batsford, 1986

Lancaster, Roy, *Travels in China: A Plantsman's Paradise*, Antique Collectors' Club, 1989

Lang Kaiyong et al, *Alpine Flowering Plants in China*, China Esperanto Press, 1997

Musgrave, Toby, et al, *The Plant Hunters*, Ward Lock, 1998

Perner, Holger, & Yibo Yuo, *Orchids of Huanglong*, China Intercontinental Press, 2007 (Chinese & English bilingual)

Valder, Peter, *The Garden Plants of China*, Weidenfeld & Nicolson, 1999

Wilson, E. H., *A Naturalist in Western China*, Cadogan Books, 1986

Wu Quanan, *Wild Flowers of Yunnan in China*, China Forestry Publishing House, 1999

Zhongjian, Chen Singchi Liu et al, *A Field Guide to the Orchids of China*, 2009 (Chinese & English bilingual)

http://www.alpinegardensociety.net

http://www.plantexplorers.com

A tropical paradise

Bao Ensheng (editor in chief) et al, *Xishuangbanna – A Nature Reserve of China*, China Forestry Publishing House, 1992

Ji Weizhi, *Birds in Yunnan*, China Forestry Publishing House, 2006 (English language version)

Liu Jia Zhu, *Flowers That Can Fly: butterflies of Yunnan, China*, China Travel & Tourism Press, 2000

Gong Xi & Zhang Qitai, *Wild Ornamental Fruit Plants from Yunnan, China*, Foreign Languages Press, 2003 (Chinese & English bilingual)

Tao Guoda, *Wild Tropical Plants in China*, 1998 (Chinese & English)

Wu Quanan, *Wild Flowers of Yunnan in China*, China Forestry Publishing House, 1999 (English)

Xishuangbanna National Reserve Administration & Yunnan Academy of Forestry Science, *Wild Tropical Plants in China*, 1998 (Chinese & English bilingual)

Magnificent tigers

Matthiessen, Peter, *Tigers in the Snow*, North Point Press, 2000

Nowell, Kristin & Xu Ling, *Taming the Tiger Trade: China's markets for wild and captive tiger products since the 1993 domestic trade ban*, A TRAFFIC East Asia report, 2007

http://assets.panda.org/downloads/ tiger_taming_colour_web_version.pdf

Tilson, Ronald, and Philip J. Nyhus (eds), *Tigers of the World: the science, politics and conservation of* Panthera tigris, Academic Press, 2nd edn, 2010

World Wildlife Federation, 'Tiger Trade: Facts & Fallacies', 13 May 2007 *http://www.worldwildlife.org/tigers /pubs/tigerfactsfallacies.pdf*

Wild Hong Kong

Bascombe, Mike, Gwyneth Johnston & Frieda Bascombe (eds), *The Butterflies of Hong Kong*, Academic Press (via A. & C. Black), 1999

Fong, T. C. W., et al, *Estuarine Organisms*, Photographic Guide Series to Hong Kong Nature (2), Hong Kong Discovery, 2005

Kemp, Derek, *Twelve Hong Kong Walks*, Oxford University Press, 1985

Lai, Vincent C. S., et al, *Hard Shore Organisms*, Photographic Guide Series to Hong Kong Nature (9), Hong Kong Discovery, 2006

Li Cunzhi, *Field Guide to Trees in Hong Kong's Countryside*, Huayu Nature Book Trade, 2008

Lui, Henry T. H., *Birdwatching in the Big City*, Photographic Guide Series to Hong Kong Nature (1), Hong Kong Discovery, 2005

Lui, Henry T. H., *Birdwatching in Farmlands and Open Fields*, Photographic Guide Series to Hong Kong Nature (7), Hong Kong Discovery, 2006

Lui, Henry T. H., *Birdwatching in Wetlands*, Photographic Guide Series to Hong Kong Nature (10), Hong Kong Discovery, 2007

Morton, Brian & John Morton, *The Sea Shore Ecology of Hong Kong*, Hong Kong University Press, 1983

Owen, Bernie, & Raynor Shaw, *Hong Kong Landscapes: Shaping the Barren Rock*, Hong Kong University Press, 2007

So, Samson N. H., & Henry T. H. Lui, *Small Wetland Creatures*, Photographic Guide Series to Hong Kong Nature (12), Hong Kong Discovery, 2007

Viney, Clive, Karen Phillips & Lam Chiu Ying, *The Birds of Hong Kong and South China*, Hong Kong Government Information Service, 2005

Walden, B. M., & S.Y. Hu, *Wild Flowers of South China and Hong Kong*, Sino-American Publishing Company

Williams, Gray A., *Rocky Shores*, Hong Kong Field Guides 1, Department of Ecology & Biodiversity, University of Hong Kong, 2003

http://www.afcd.gov.hk/eindex.html Agricultural, Fisheries & Conservation Department, Hong Kong

http://www.hkbws.org.hk Hong Kong Bird Watching Society

http://www.hkoutdoors.com

Precipitous peaks

Huang Youyi et al, *Anhui Mount Huangshan and the Hui Culture*, Foreign Languages Press, 2006

Xiang Xiaoyang, *Huangshan Photo Travel Guide*, China Photographic Publishing House, 2008

INDEX

Entries in bold refer to images

Maps appear on the following pages:
12, 28, 46, 54, 62, 74, 90, 106, 122, 138, 150, 166, 172, 177, 178, 180, 182, 185